Meet the Fokkens

Martine en Louise Fokkens

Meet the Fokkens

At the Red Light District

Aspekt Publishers

Meet the Fokkens

© 2015 Uitgeverij ASPEKT
© Martine en Louise Fokkens

Amersfoortsestraat 27, 3769 AD Soesterberg, Nederland
info@uitgeverijaspekt.nl - http://www.uitgeverijaspekt.nl

Photo cover: Charise Blokdijk
Cover: Mark Heuveling
Interlining: Maarten Bakker
Translated by: Ellen van den Broek

ISBN: 9789461537010
NUR: 740

All rights reserved. No part of these pages, either text or image may be used for any purpose other than personal use. Therefore, reproduction, modification, storage in a retrieval system or retransmission, in any form or by any means, electronic, mechanical or otherwise, for reasons other than personal use, is strictly prohibited without prior written permission.

Table of Contents

The Women of Life	9
Amsterdam 1970	10
My Own Little Bordello at the Amsterdam Koestraat	12
Two Pimps /Koestraat Amsterdam	14
Hotel Kees Stappe, Amsterdam Koestraat	16
A Romance at the Red Light District and Angie Leaves the Redlight Lifestyle, Amsterdam 1960s	17
Amsterdam. Piet the Know-It-All. Oude Nieuwstraat	19
The Spanker O.Z. Voorburgwal Amsterdam	21
The Reverend Wants to Get Spanked. Koestraat 1970s Amsterdam	23
The Bijenkorf Pimp and the Sailors, Oudezijds Voorburgwal, Amsterdam	25
An Urgent Need with SOS in my Pants, Amsterdam 1970s Koestraat	28
The Fur Coat Man, Amsterdam, Koestraat 14	30
Moos and Roos, Mister Pielemoos (Mister Willy). Koestraat 14, Amsterdam	32
The Madame and Housekeeper, late 1970s	34
Tien acherlove with Real Emotion	38
Frits Never Enough? (Chapter missing)	39
The Taxi Pimp, the 1960s O.Z Voorburgswal Amsterdam	41
The Weekend Pimp (Sunday nights) O.Z Voorburgwal	42
Odet Smoked a Joint and I Tried it Too, O.Z Voorburgwal, Amsterdam 1960s	45
Proposing a New Beginning, Almere 2013	48
The Criminal Investigation Department, Warmoesstraat O.Z. Voorburgwal, Amsterdam	50
His Mother's Pimp. Koestraat 14 Amsterdam	53
Sheila and her Argentinian Pimp, Koestraat 14. Amsterdam. Sheila and Jordy First Sequel	56
Sequel 2. Sheila and Jordy. Koestraat 14, Amsterdam	58
Four Balls yet we Peep at the Red Light District	61
Songs in and out of the Whore House	62
Sensation at the Brothel. O.Z. Voorburgwal Amsterdam, 1960s	63
To Cut and Shag. Amsterdam Koestraat	66
To Pay for Love	68
The Turd. Amsterdam Koestraat	69
Abdoel the Regular, Amsterdam Koestraat	71

Meeting Someone New, and I could become a Pimp. Amsterdam O.Z. Voorburgwal	73
We booked a Hotel at the Geldersekade	76
Mister S(cr)ewing Threat met us at our Brothel. The Amsterdam City Centre. Koestraat 14	79
Drinking a Cup of Coffee with Loeki. Albert Cuyp, Amsterdam.	81
Loekie, Amsterdam. Off to the whore house	83
A Night out on the Town with Loeki and Loes. And I can become a Pimp. O.Z. Voorburgwal.	85
To the Eland canal. Ouwezijds. Nanne you can't have my Pimp.	87
At the Oudezijdsvoorburgwal 97 Amsterdam October 1960s	91
Amsterdam Ceintuurbaan	93
The Sequel to the Return Journey. Coming home with Wimpie, Amsterdam Ceintuurbaan 237	95
	101
Koestraat, Jan Sigaar (cigar) 19 Amsterdam	103
Oude Nieuwstraat 5, Amsterdam 19 Amsterdam City Centre	108
The Wimp. Koestraat 14 Amsterdam	110
When the Road worker Temporarily Became a Male Ballerina, Koestraat	112
The Man with the Rubber Boots	135
Timid	136
At the Red Light District	137
The Red Light	138
We don't want to leave You	139
The Old Dog	141
Wank the Little donkey	142
Off to the Whorehouse, 1970s. Ouwenieuwstraat	144
A Pimp for an Hour. Pimp Dik was entranced? O.Z. Voorburgwal	147
The Carpet Beater. Koestaat, Amsterdam city center.	149
Pietje and the Schoolteacher, Koestraat 19	151
The Man who was Crazy about Bonbons, Roestraat Amsterdam	153
Oudenieuwstraat at Kittie's place	154
The Shopping Mall. Jantje Fish IJmijden, July 2011	157
The Great Wobbler. Amsterdam Koestraat.	159
We go out Clubbing and get some Extra Attention from a Woman. Amsterdam O.Z. Voorburgwal	162
My Pimp was having the Time of his Life. Amsterdam 1960s O.Z. Voorburgwal	164
The Brothel, 1972 O.Z.	

Back to Work O.Z. Harrijet 1972	167
Stoned as a Shrimp +- 65 O.Z. Voorburgwal Amsterdam Sloestraat	169
My Jatmous, I can't turn Him down. O.Z. Voorburgwal Amsterdam, 1963	173
The Fucker, Amsterdam Koestraat 1975	175
Meringue. Ouwe Nieuwstraat, Chrissie	177
Kees is in the Mood	179
Our New Place, Amsterdam	182
Pimp Turd, Amsterdam	186

 # The women of life

They are the women of life, yes they: are the women working at, the Red Light District.
She worked to survive facing it all; strolling through the Red-Light life.
Despised, disregarded, yet also praised.
Yes, they were crowned by life.
Those are the women; yes the women of the Red-Light life; yes the Red-Light life.
They did it for: food.
And to survive.
It is what they do, the women of:
The red-light life.

Louise.

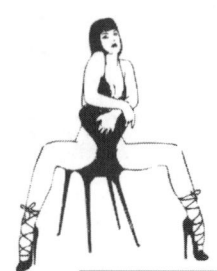 # Amsterdam 1970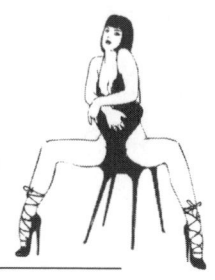

From the Oudezijdsvoorburgwal number 1970 to the Oude Nieuwstraat 4, which will be my new place. How exciting, it feels like I am going to kindergarten for the first time. It is situated between the Singel and the Spui. Yes it is time to move to my new brothel. I grab my bag with all my sex toys and run downstairs. To my BMW I go, I step on the gas and race through town towards the Singel, and make a right towards the Oudenieuwstraat. I immediately find a space in the ally before the AQU factory called de Varta, where people were already at work. I grab my bag and all my stuff and go out to find Aunt Ernie at number 4, where I ring the bell for my key. A window is opened and out comes Aunt Ernie shouting; ah are you the new girl Tien, good then I will go grab your key. I wait a minute and there she comes throwing down my key saying she will bring me coffee in a minute. Thank you. Ah now the fun can begin. I walk inside through the hallway and notice the creaking of the floorboards underneath my feet. On my left is the lavatory and beside it a small granite countertop which used to serve as a sink, with a small curtain before it and an IUD and a bin for used condoms. Behind was a storage room, I peek inside but find it too dark and quickly close the door. I have seen enough, it is time to change and get to work. I am wearing a red dress. I open the curtain and immediately a man steps in. We agree on the price and I start unbuttoning a few of the buttons on my red dress. Tell me, what is your name? Huub. Well isn't that nice, why don't you put your clothes on the chair. I get started with the condom, I have to do it right otherwise it will crack. There, Huub is ready and we both lie down on the bed, immediately sinking in. Down into the old spiral bed. Where we do it. I must say, it is exhausting, having sex in a hole in the bed. The bed squeaks and cracks and squeaking and cracking we climax at the same time? Hurray.

Martine.

 # My Own Little Bordello at the Amsterdam Koestraat

Good morning all. We need to hurry today; fast fast fast. We race towards the Koestraat in the new market neighbourhood. As we arrive the new tenant is already waiting for us with her pimp. She wanted to live on the first floor and immediately wanted to join the Red-Light lifestyle. So it was a done deal. She was a robust black-haired woman from Belgium, with a wonderful rack. Lieke was ready to go, already wearing her sex clothes. Well there we go. I opened the door and together we walked up the stairs to the first floor. All four of us. I gave her the key and gracefully she opened the door to her new place. Lieke paid her bail as her pimp Vic immediately went to work. She thanked us; and asked; can I immediately start working Loes? Of course you can! Well scram then; out you go. Whatever you want, see you later Lieke. We walked down the stairs into our own little sex rooms and opened the blinds. Let the men come! Tien made a pot of coffee. Suddenly we hear a noise on the stairs and a door closes with a bang. Ah it is Lieke; who stormed in. Alé it is wonderful here. Do you also want a cup, Tien asked. Of course. Lieke drank her coffee and left for the streets. She looked spunky wearing that tight red skirt, red sweater with a wide neck, and those wonderful long legs. There she went, strolling with her high heels on down the street. It only took her five minutes before she scored. After that Lieke met many men. We were ecstatic as we met some studs as well that day. At the end of the day we score a gypsy boy. He is looking good; with jet black eyes, shiny black hair; wearing nothing but gold. Well, bring it on. Dango gives us a hug and pays us well. He often visits after he has made some money. The gypsy boy fantasizes about everything, and boy has he come up with something today. Today he is here to abduct us. Of course we said no. He wants us to move in with his gypsy family. He wants them to accept it. Dango takes of his clothes and sings to us a gypsy love song. He gets to his knees, hugs us and loudly tells us to listen because we have to come with him. Tien looks at me and nods; I grab a condom because it is time. We grab Dingo. He struggles. Tien says, you are not here to abduct anyone mister. And alternately we wank the lovely gypsy boy. He came and for the moment loses all his sexual tensions. He enjoyed it. Afterwards he left. At the door he shouted, bye for now. Tomorrow we go at it again.

Louise.

Two Pimps
Amsterdam Koestraat

Lieke had two pimps and loved them both.

Good morning all, there we go again. Hurry up Loes, I am excited to go. Do we have enough clean laundry to take with us to the bordello, I have put everything in the car. And off we went to Amsterdam. Soon we arrive. Lieke had been working with us for a couple of weeks and was doing well on our first floor. She had many regular customers. It was the end of September and today it was Friday. So the weekend could begin, and all of a sudden there he was, a large man, waving and screaming at our front door. So I open the door; and ask what is going on; are you looking for something sir? Yes I am. I need my bitch; what bitch? The Belgian one. You know, Lieke. O; Lieke, but isn't she with Vic. Well listen to me lady, that is none of my concern. She is and will be my bitch. Understood. Yes it is all fine with me. I am not in the mood for this, he is disrupting my business. I grab the key of Lieke's place and tell the drunk I will take a look. I rang the bell and opened the door, the drunk, however, followed me and is standing a little too close. The bastard smelled like alcohol, he must have emptied a can or two. So I call Lieke – Lieke. And it works. The door opens and Lieke looks at me. Sleepily she asks me what is wrong. Your man is here. Man. And the drunk bastard immediately responds and runs up the stairs. And Lieke had nothing left to say. He told her to go in. I called for her asking it if was okay. Yes Loes, its fine.

Louise.

Hotel Kees Stappe
Amsterdam Koestraat

It's okay. I continued my work and after a little while I heard a lot of noise from upstairs. I thought someone fell down the stairs. They cried and laughed at the same time. To my astonishment I saw Lieke coming down the stairs with a man on each arm. Hi Loes, we will go out for a drink, the three of us: at Hotel Kees at the Kloveniers Burgwal. Well have fun. And as they walked out I saw them turn the corner having all sorts of fun. This had been going on for years with Lieke and her first man. And Vic, her second, would have to accept it, otherwise they would beat each other senseless. Lieke sustained her two pimps. And always kept them close. And on set times she had to give away her earned money; to the drunk pimp. Yes she did have to do that. Especially since his motto was, if you won't give it nicely, I will take it with force. So she did what she had to do and settled it with booze and fun, after which the pimp life with her second pimp Vic could continue. Having Kees' bar around the corner of the Koestraat, Lieke was often to be found hanging at the bar and stapled to her stool, enjoying life. She met many of her clients there. She was a good prostitute, and at Hotel Kees it was always fun. Kees was one hell of a guy, but that's enough for today. I am still my own boss. So pack your bags and go, it is time for bed. Goodbye.

A Romance at the Red Light District and Angie leaves the Red-light Lifestyle, Amsterdam 1960s

Angie fell in love at the Red Light District; what if something like that happens to you. She lost her heart to a somewhat younger man. He was a student, which meant he had to study hard. Angie was in love. Head over heels in love. She lived for that man alone, and his name was Hans. At first he came once a month as a customer; he fell in love and came more often after that. In the end he came once a week. Even the girls at the bordello began to notice. And all of us said, during a cup of coffee, gee Angie you look excited. You have bedroom eyes; are you in love? Hans visits twice a week. What are we going to do; Angie blushed and said she was sorry. I had no idea this could happen to me. Hans makes me extremely horny. I am head over heels in love with him. I am living on a cloud. And we laughed and laughed. Angie, you have our blessing. We would love to experience that again. Being in love. Yes, wonderful, the girls said. Say Angie, is Hans any good. He is great. Those Dutch men know how to get around. Well, in your case we always thought, once a brown dick, always a brown dick. No, of course not, Hans is wonderful. Color makes no difference. You are a lucky girl Angie; how are you going to handle things with this guy. What are you going to do? After all, you also have three beautiful half-blood children. They are fun and beautiful. Yes girl, I never thought this would happen. It could happen to anyone. And still I am really in love with Hansie. Well then go for it! It is going to be hard, despite everything. It will be difficult to let go of all these familiar things. But my children will not suffer from this. We will solve this as adults. Well, good luck with that. Girls, the time to chatter is over. There are studs outside. Let's see who can score one first. It was a busy day at the brothel Doors opening and closing. And for today I am done. I cleaned my room, changed and said goodbye to all the girls. Grabbed my car and drove home. Angie, finally did decide to take off with her beloved Hans. Angie left the Red-Light lifestyle. She moved from Amsterdam to somewhere else. They even got married. It was very romantic, they even got a daughter. I lost sight of Angie, which was a shame. However, that is how it goes in life. Unfortunately the good old days will never come back. I guess we have to wait until some other time. For today I'm done. The Sandman is calling me. With lots of love; till next time.

Louise

Amsterdam Piet the Know-It-All
Oude Nieuwstraat

Today I left home a little early because of a birthday I have to go to tonight. I leave two hours early. Because I want to arrive at the party in time. Now let's see what I can score today. I entered my booth and looked at the ally. And yes, a young man approached, he was about 28 years old and asked me how much it cost. Well, for you my friend 50 gulden (Dutch currency before the Euro). All right. Come on in. We walked towards my room and Piet hung his jacket on the coatrack. A nice room you have here madam. Yes it is nice, isn't it. Suddenly Piet hesitated, and I felt something was wrong. It did not feel right. Odd. I told Piet to pay up. To pay; yes of course I will pay. And hurry up will you. Well Madam I though you said I didn't have to pay. What the hell was that? I mean I am a beautiful boy right. Are you serious, you can always find someone else to light your fire. You might be beautiful and all, but don't act so stupid. You don't have to be here you know. Better leave then. And make it quick. Oh no madam I do want to stay. Well, all right then. Piet grabbed his wallet and paid me 100 gulden. Immediately I put his money away. Alright then, we can begin. Suddenly Piet wasn't so bold anymore as he quietly enjoyed what was happening to him. I caressed Piet and massaged his dick up and down, and his balls. And that is how Piet travelled to seventh heaven and back, enjoying it immensely. Piet relaxed, jumped out of bed and got dressed. Well, madam. Thank you, it was worth my money. I apologize once again, and until the next time. Bye Piet, until next time. Piet left the ally, I cleaned my room, put on my party dress and want to the party. Happy birthday. Hurray.

Martine.

The Spanker O.Z. Voorburgwal Amsterdam

Today I was in early, sitting on my throne, when suddenly a man stood in front of my window. Hello young lady, may I ask you something. Why of course, come on in. Tell me. Well, I have a slightly uncommon question. Tell me. Well, it's like this; like what. Sir if you don't know what it is, how am I supposed to know. I can't do anything with that. So if you give me some money up front we can go to my room. Oh, I'm sorry he said, and immediately grabbed his wallet giving me 50 gulden. We walked up to my room and the man put his belongings on a chair. And then he told me what he wanted. He took his coat and from the inside he took a stack of money. I believe they came right from the bank. That or he had ironed them. The man sat down on the edge of my bed with the stack of bills. He looked at me and asked me if I wanted to sit down beside him. I did what he asked and sat close to him. Now I needed to find out what he wanted for that kind of money, and how I would be able to get it. It wasn't very nice of him holding the cash right in front of me. Now hurry Loes. I looked at him. So, what are we going to do? In my hand I have 1000 gulden for you. Well great, bring it on. No, I will give you 100 gulden each time. Oh and why is that? You are being punished by me; oh why? I didn't do anything wrong. Yes you did, you do not listen to me if I ask you something. Or when I tell you what you need to do for me. You ignore it all. I know nothing of such things sir. Well, I do, and it bothers me. And now I'm done with you. If you continue to disobey me I will spank you, after which you get a 100 gulden bill of my stack. And now I would like to start; so naughty young lady, go stand in the corner. Yes sir, but first let me get my 100 gulden. No, no young lady, first you get spanked and hurry up because once again you aren't listening to me. Quickly I walked to the corner and got spanked. Afterwards I got my 100 gulden and put it away. And the man protested, you have taken one too many. Again you disobey me. Not true, we have been talking for ages before we got here and it is my time. Oh is that true young lady? Well then go back to your corner because you won't listen anyway. So I stood in another corner. And he spanked me once again, after which I took another bill. And this continued for some time. Sometimes I held a newspaper before my bum. He protested but it all turned out fine. And all his money was spent. Afterwards he sat down quietly. I gave him something to drink. Satisfied he said goodbye and left. I cleaned up and took care of my flaming bum.

Louise.

The Reverend wants to get Spanked.
Koestraat 1970s Amsterdam

Here we go again. To eat or be eaten. So we work today, because the money won't earn itself. It was bleak outside. Fortunately I was sitting on my high stool; close to the heater, in the window. Dammit, after an hour there were still no customers. Well then I would just have to try a little harder, because I have had enough. I jumped of my stool, grabbed my warm coat and stood at my door in order to bring in customers. Still, the street was abandoned. On to the streets we go. Finally a man entered the ally. Maybe I was lucky. He was a sturdy and very tall man. Completely dressed in black. Quickly I strolled over to him; he looked at me from under his hat. How can I help you? Will you come with me? Come with you where? Well, to the brothel of course. I am sorry, but I don't have much time. I have an appointment, and might be late. Of course not, we'll make it a quickie. Well, all right then; together we walked back to my place. To the first room where we hung our coats. He asked me how much it cost. How much can you spare? Are you sure you don't want to stay longer. I might little girl. Because what I want might take a little longer. Sure, let's do that. He offered me 75 gulden, which I quickly put away. He sat down. So tell me young man, what do you do for a living. Why are you wearing such dark clothes?

All dressed up in your black suit. Snow-white shirt. I need this suit and shirt for work. I am a reverend. Oh but of course. Well, reverend, what are we going to do. I will tell you what. I would like to get spanked by you. All right. Let the good times begin. Reverend, why don't you lie down on your stomach? I grabbed my carpet-beater and started to spank him softly, after which I hit him a little harder. A little harder and then a little softer. His bum began to turn red, so it was time to lose the carpet-beater. Now turn around reverend. Get of the bed. I sat at the edge of the bed and pulled him across my lap and spanked him hard. And the reverend shouted, good, keep going, harder, harder. I deserve it. Harder, for I have sinned and feel remorse. Harder, harder, I must be punished. And so I spanked him several more times. But my hand began to feel sore so I ended it. Reverend, you have been properly punished for today. Quickly he got up, and there he was dressed in his black suit and hat. Right in front of me. Thanks so much little girl. I better go now, maybe I can still make it to my appointment in time. He looked at me from under his hat one more time and disappeared into the crowds, as I continued my work.

Louise

The Bijenkorf Pimp and the Sailors, Oudezijds Voorburgwal

There we go again today. Into the car; and from the south of Amsterdam to the Red Light District. We raced towards the Voorburgwal, parked the car, and entered our brothel. We were greeted by Leen, our Madame. Hi girls, I have brought you something to drink and eat. I am going for a walk. Okay Leen. Bye ladies, see you later. Quickly we arranged our rooms, and within ten minutes we were standing at the door, wearing our sexy outfits in order to make some money. The weather was great, we enjoyed it. Soon we scored. A group of sailors approached us. They looked very handsome in their uniforms. There were four of them, talking to each other. Two stayed while the other two left. They agreed to meet at the Old Sailors Bar at the Achterburgwal. The famous sailor bar. With our sailors we walked to our brothel and closed the door. We grabbed their hats and put them on admiring ourselves in the mirror. Everyone went to their own room and now the fun could begin. I put away his hat and the sailor neatly put his clothes on the chair. He put the money on the countertop and we danced to the music on the radio. Our sailors hadn't seen the shore in quite some time, so my sailor wanted to take things slow. He asked me if I had some erotic books so he could look at the pictures. And he wanted to try out some positions. I grabbed a few books and he eagerly began to go through them. Say Loes, how about these two positions; looks like fun. How about we immediately begin our sexual gymnastics. I would love to. First my sailor wanted to have sex doggy style. And, as a trained sailor he moved up and down. He wanted to recreate the pictures of the entire book. Enthusiastically I said, of course sailor. Why don't you let me pick the next one. Soon he was lying on his back, and then he was back on his knees. With two firm thrusts the sexual gymnastics came to an end. The sailor fell down beside me, snickering. I jumped of the bed and got dressed again; soon I heard my sister arrive with her stud. They waited in the front room. My sailor jumped into action as well and before I knew it he was fully dressed and standing in front of me. I opened the door and once again there were the four of us. We waved our sailors goodbye and went back inside. We talked about our sailors and returned to our doors. Loes, look who is coming our way; where I don't see anything. Look closely. Oh I see. The Bijenkorf pimp. And there he was standing right in front of us boasting about how he would soon get a promotion at the Bijenkorf, after which he would become even more important. Then his wife would also stop being a prostitute. Afterwards they would enter the hotel and catering industry. Well, that is a bright-looking future Dirk. If you try hard you can stay. And he did try saying he thought I was a hot bitch. Can I come with you? No not anymore. At first it was fine. But you are a pimp now yourself, and your wife is a few blocks away. We don't do that to one of our own. You do understand that do you? No I don't understand. I think you are a hot bitch, and I am crazy about you. When we are together I will take good care of you. Dirk, you comedian, stop it would you. You are trying to get me to work for you. I am taken. One pimp is enough for me. Now stop and go take a hike because my pimp will be here any minute now. And then things could get really ugly. Bye Dirk. Finally he hesitantly left. I have seen Dirk walk by occasionally, after many years he did enter the hotel and catering industry. And according to some he is living in a large house at the beach with his wife and children. Well that's it for today. I am going home to watch television with my children tonight.

Louise and Martine.

An urgent need with SOS in my pants, Amsterdam 1970s Koestraat

Good afternoon. It is urgent madam. Oh?; yes; I have sos and need to come with you now. Well, what is so urgent then young man? Well, it's just. Just what? Yes, Yes I have sos. O; I am in dire need. Do you need to pee? No it's not that I want you; I want. You want what? Come on kid tell me. And then I looked at him closely. Oh now I get it. Why didn't you say so. His jeans was completely filled up and his fly was about to burst open. Do you want to go inside with me Thijs? Yes madam. You do have to pay first you know. Aught for naught, and a penny change. He looked at me and yelled: yes;yes; of course, now hurry madam, and he grabbed my arm and said come on quick; quickly now I have sos sos. Yes calm down. Together we ran down the hall to my room. Thijs grabbed his money and I knew what to do with it. He threw his coat on the floor. I barely had time to take of my coat. His gentlemen was calling me. And his dick shone as he put his own condom on and started to masturbate. He pulled me close and once again yelled come on madam it is so urgent, come on I have sos sos. Yes Thijs that's fine. I grabbed his sos and yanked at it as if there was no tomorrow. I even got a sore arm. And I called out to him sos, sos, until Thijs finally came. Well that was something madam. Yes it was; your sos was in dire straits. Smiling Thijs walked outside. I waved his sos goodbye, cleaned up and walked back to my stool in the window, waiting for another stud. I could continue for hours today. Goodbye.

Louise

The Fur Coat Man
Amsterdam, Koestraat 14

II want two girls. Winter clothing is back. The pea soup was ready. And my sister and I were standing in front of our bordello; at the Koestraat 14. It was cold out and temperatures were below zero. So we wore our fur coats and hats. The pavement had been cleared of ice and the Red Light District was open for business. We were messing around with our neighbor when a man walked by and asked if he could ask us a question. Of course sir, you can always ask. You are standing here, the three of you. But I would like to come with two of you, is that possible? Sure you can always go with the twins. She is our neighbor from across the street Well girls, I'm off. Duty calls. My pimp needs me to get to work and offer him our weekly fuck as dessert. You are a lucky girl. Enjoy it. I will. And our neighbor ran up the stairs and entered her own house. And my sister and I focused on the stud in front of us and walked to our room. We were standing there with our fur coats still on, and he was smirking at us. Tien said, come on Loes, something has to happen now. We look like two stone pillars. Tien took matters into her own hands and allows Pjear to get his wallet. Loyally he offered us both 125 gulden. So we began to take our coats of. And Pjear immediately began to panic. It scared the death out of me. What the hell was that? No, No, that is not what I meant. Well what do you mean? You look amazing in your coats. Keep 'em on. Whatever you want. Pjear took off his clothes; and said; why don't you lay down on the bed. One on each side. And I will lie down in the middle. And so it happened. He didn't have enough hands, constantly plucking and feeling our coats, from one to the other. It really turned him on. Soon he was ready to go; so it became a quick fuck surrounded by fur. Afterwards Pjear collapsed. Girls I have enjoyed this tremendously. I can't go for another round today. Well, Pjear we have had enough as well we chimed in. Try again next time. Well, girls, I am extremely satisfied and will often dream of when I will be able to visit you again. Before Pjear left us he touched our fur coats once more and took off. We took our coats off, cleaned the place and were ready to go home, completely covered in fur. We looked at each other and couldn't stop laughing. We took off, to come back tomorrow.

Louise and Martine.

Moos and Roos,
Mister Pielemoos (Mister Willy)
Koestraat 14, Amsterdam

Good morning Moos. How are you doing Roos? Hi Roosa; are you excited about today? Excited about what? I will tell you. Now I am curious, do tell Moos. Why are you showing of that big bag? What is in it? I will show you in a minute. You do have to come in Moos, because this won't get us anywhere. All right, I will come with you. Now and no later; great Moos. Soon you will have your hands free; for when you go shopping at the Kalverstraat. That is a great idea Roosa; yes flowers on your hat. And together we walked through the hallway towards my room. Moos placed the large bag on the bed. Put his clothes on the chair. Got his wallet and paid me 100 gulden. Is this enough Roos?; for now it is; Moos. We will see; Roos. Moos got his bag and opened it. I have brought you flowers Roos, just for you. Because after all this time I still love you. They are beautiful red roses Moos. I feel all warm and tingly inside. I blush. Yes, my dear Roos, that is why I give you red roses. So we can blush together. I put the roses in some water. And Moos started messing with me again. Roos close your eyes. Why; Moos. Just wait and see. I closed my eyes. And Moos began to chant all sorts of hocus pocus. Open your eyes. Okay Moos, and there he was, standing in the middle of the room with his willy in his hand. Wow

Moos, you sure performed some magic in here. You can go on tour with that performance. Moos couldn't stop laughing. Yeah Moos, that size means you have to pay extra. Okay Roos; he took his wallet and offered me another 50 gulden. I grabbed a condom and magically put it on his large willy. We fell on the bed and our magic trick began. I firmly held his willy; and with a rocking movement Moos went faster and faster. It didn't go in all the way, and that was fine because Moos was done. And he loved it and had enjoyed it. He got dressed and magically made a box of cherry bonbons appear from his jacket. Thank you Rose; I had loads of fun. Thank you Moos. We performed some great magic here today didn't we? We sure did. Bye bye. Bye Mister Pielemoos (Willy).

Louise.

The Madame and Housekeeper late 1970s

Good evening all. After I had spent the entire day cleaning the brothel, and offered the girls who were working and living with us in our small little house, something to drink and eat I went to bed after supper. Afterwards I had regained my strength and was ready for business. To make some money. I was ready to go. So the fun could begin, and as I stuck my head out the door I noticed many men were roaming the streets. I decided to walk around the block to stretch my legs. I strolled from the Koestraat to the Achterburgwal. It was nice out. However, a sweater was not unnecessary. I was feeling restless so I decided to walk around; and that is how I found myself at the Bloedstraat, after which I walked via the Kloveniersburgwal back to our brothel. There I saw my twin sister talking to a man and a woman. They greeted me from far. When I came closer I immediately saw; it was Oukie with her new husband Elie. My sister told me they were looking for a place to stay. What a coincidence, we have a small apartment available on the second floor and you are free to move in anytime. Because I have cleaned it top to bottom today. Can we look at it? Of course. Tien will you grab the keys. They are in the kitchen drawer. Tien immediately went out to get them. The four of us walked up the stairs. We showed them the inside of the place and Oukie and Elie loved it. Afterwards we agreed to meet again the day after tomorrow. Then they will bring all their belongings. Say Tien, I was ready for some customers but I am done for the day. Well, Loes let's get the hell out of here then. We made our last rounds and went home. I knew Oukie from when I was a teenager. She came from a difficult home. Because of circumstances he hadn't always been raised at home. She went from foster family to foster family. So it wasn't always easy for her. Her mother also used to live in the Red Light District area. At some point she was with a pimp, someone she had been with for years. It was an on, off kind of relationship. Oukie joined her mother at the Red Light District when she was a little older. And also met her mother's pimp Gees. After some time Oukie left with her mother's pimp and together they got a daughter. For quite some time everything worked out fine for them and their daughter. And all of a sudden everything changed. Oukie also ended up in the window at the Red Light District. In a brothel at the Voorburg burgwal. There, me and my sister often met Oukie. And Gees often came by on his way to a brothel to pick up Oukie's money. She was a fine prostitute. Often she would be able to get a lot of money from men; she was a lucky whore that one. Suddenly Oukie was gone. Moved. And, she didn't stay with Gees. As before she was strolling down the

Red Light District with some guy at her arm, named Elie. And next week they move in above the brothel. And afterwards she rented a room downstairs to continue her work as a prostitute. They were fun times. Oukie was doing a great job and had loads of fun. Elie came from Indonesia. And our sitter for the night was Euchen; he also came from Indonesia, so the two got along just fine. Often they made delicious Indonesian meals in our little kitchen at the brothel. Euchen was an amazing cook. Oukie lived on the second floor for several years and worked downstairs. Occasionally Elie became restless and would stay out a night or two. Though he always picked up Oukie's money. In the end we found out that Elie was in contact with his first bitch again. So Oukie couldn't take it anymore. So they often fought, including the usual swear fights. So the whole neighborhood could enjoy it. Afterwards we all went upstairs to calm both of them down. And that's basically how life continued. At one point Oukie was offered a place in the east of Amsterdam. She lived there for many years. Oukie and Elie got a daughter together. Their wish had been fulfilled. My sister and I visited the baby many times. She was a beautiful baby. And her oldest daughter also moved back home. Fortunately. After that Oukie moved again; we stayed in touch over the phone. And after we moved we lost track of one another. We haven't spoken to each other in years. So every now and again we cleaned apartments. That's life in a brothel. People come and go. And that is how it will remain. And now the two of us need to go home as well.

Louise.

Tien acherlove with real emotion

Although you were never faithful to me. How on earth is it possible for me to still love you? You gave me your word, you made a promise. I was all in. What did you do? You have to work for it. It is not too late. To love someone; it doesn't cost much. Don't be afraid to believe in it. What has come from two people. A new life; came from love. That is how our children and grandchildren are born with my love. Where were you; hard as stone, cold as ice. You no longer fool me. You wasted your love and warmth; for your own children and grandchildren as a coward. And the love and warmth you still long for. The love another never gave you. Your children and grandchildren. They still love you. So step over that threshold; forget your cowardly pride. Make it work; as long as you are still able to at your age. Look your children in the eye. Show them you are sorry. Feel remorse. Show them it is still possible. Because we all still loved you. Take a chance, make everyone feel alive once more. It's because I, the same girl, the teenager who fell in love; with you, my first, together we were a couple in love. Still love you so much. And will remain true to you for the rest of my life. My Tien acterlove with real emotion. For always and forever!

Louise.

Frits Never Enough

Emie was working at the Oude Nieuwstraat. She asks if I would like a cup of coffee, I say I would love some. I walk upstairs and take a break. I ring her doorbell and she pulls the cord hanging down the stairs. As I walk to her place I can smell the coffee, it smells really good. Emie whisks some milk and hands me a cup of coffee. Her sowing machine is on the table, she has made some lovely clothes for all types of dolls. Immediately I order some of what she has made for my own girls. After my coffee duty calls so I walk down the stairs and close my door. Soon someone approaches me and asks me how much it cost. We agree on the price and he joins me inside, talking all about what he wants to do. Easy there fella, that would take a couple of days. Say what's your name anyway? It's Frits. Well, that name certainly suits you. Okay, so you do have to pay up before we can get started. Of course madam here you go, thank you Frits. Why don't you put your clothes over there, then I will unbutton my dress. Frits walks over and begins to feel me up, enjoying every second of it. It is really getting him in the mood. Slowly we walk over to the bed. Frits says to me; I will get you properly laid. Soon he fucks me like there is no tomorrow. It is mind-blowing. Thanks Tien, once again we reached the finish line, he says while he begins to laugh. Being with me had made his day. Well, I think it's time for me to go. Duty calls. I will see you soon girl. Bye Tien.

Martine

 # The Taxi Pimp, the 1960s O.Z. Voorburgswal Amsterdam

A pimp who works hard; yes they do exist. How could we forget? Well, fortunately we didn't. His name was Enkie, a temporary taxi driver. He also drove meat to the butchers in town; as a delivery. He was related to us. Enkie's wife also worked at the Voorburgwal for two years, her name was Rijke. And the best of it all is that Rijke was only a prostitute for two years as well. During those years they saved some money; so they could start something. Isn't that nice. Too bad some men and women forget how they once lived. One as a pimp, and the other as just another prostitute. The people they borrowed money from, and the friends they had, they ignore. My sister and I always had fun with Rijke during those years of prostitution. Together we often got many customers. And all of a sudden she didn't come back. They bought a nice house with lots of land, so they could bring their hobby to life. They were crazy about horses. It was great; they had enough room. And Rijke owned a large vegetable garden. And trees filled with fruit. Visiting her during the summer always left us with bags filled with vegetables and fruit. It's a shame, my sister and I miss the good old days. The 1960s, the three of us living the life at the Red Light District; we will never lose those days.

Louise

The Weekend Pimp
(Sunday nights)
O.Z. Voorburgwal

He was a regular of one of my colleagues. Tina worked at the same brothel as I. Tonight, both of us had already seen some regulars; so the night was going well. We took a cup of tea and talked. Afterwards we went back out; to continue our work. And in comes this fine gentleman. Tina began to snicker. What is that all about Tina? Customer? Well what did you expect? All right, fine by me. Jet black hair and fortunately a little over 18 years old, ran past us and walked through the side door. Tina looked shocked. Afterwards she walked to the back. Closed the door. Snickering through the hallway, the both of them, into her sex room, and the fun could begin. Soon I met a customer; a quickie; another wank, and still no Tina. I was getting impatient; and went to check things out. I walked to her room and called, Tina are you okay? They didn't make a sound so I pounded on the door. Tina Tina; and then I heard a sleepy voice. We're all right; just romantically fell asleep. That's great, now get going, it is time to go! Okay Loes, we are on our way. And there they were, the petulant couple. They smooched for a while and the guy took off. Well, Tina you look excited. You think? Hey Loes. I am in love. As long as it doesn't cost you a lot of money. Well I don't hope so. I can use my cash. And need it to sustain my kids. Making out is fine. But taking me out won't do. I hope so kid. We'll see Loes. Time will tell. Well, think of it like this, as long as it is fun and you are in love, it's all fine with me. Whatever you want. Next weekend he will come to my house. Ah see that's where it all starts. As long as you have fun. I can't wait. Well start the countdown. Tina do keep yourself together tonight all right. Sure, I will stay for another hour to make some money. Okay, I am sorry for you Tina, but I am almost done for the day; in half an hour I will leave if I have no other customers. We'll see. I leaned against the door; it was a wonderful night. And look who came around the corner. Sorba the Greek. All dressed in white. Tight pants and no underwear. You could see his entire cock sticking out. Walking through the Red Light District made him super horny. He walked past us with a smile. Well, I wonder what will happen next. And suddenly he was standing right in front of me; staring me down. Well, well Sorba you look particularly sexy tonight. Come dance with me. Right now; just the two of us. He grabbed me by the arm and pulled me inside. Into my room. Hey Sorba take it easy. You need to pay first. No, I don't have to do that no? Well why wouldn't you? But I am a handsome Greek. Sure you are but that makes no difference to me. Nice; try. He grabbed a stack of bills and handed me 75 gulden. I quickly put it away. Let's get this party started. We danced through my room. He took his shirt of. Fly open, and out came his Greeky. There we go; I quickly put a condom on. He softly massaged my breasts. Suddenly he became a little grabby, viciously squeezing my nipples. I immediately took his wrists and pushed him on the bed. Hey easy now you. You won't do that again. Understood? Sorry Sorry. I sat down beside him on the bed, and kept wanking his sneaky Greeky. And suddenly Sorba had come. Put on his white ensemble and said goodbye; lots of love; until the next time. Bye Sorba. Afterwards I quickly took off. I was done for the day. With Tina it all started well; the romance. Many weekends he spent at her place. In the end he often needed money, so he became her pimp. He never had enough cash. She saw him for quite some time. Suddenly she discovered that during the week he spent time with his wife and kid. He told Tina he was out of town for work from Monday till Friday. He told his wife he had to work out of town each weekend. It all sounded plausible to both women. So he kept messing around. He did, however, always come home to his wife with lots of money. So he tried to keep going as long as he could. His double life destroyed him; both women turned their backs on him. And he was forced to live his life on his own. And that's how he stopped being a weekend pimp. And it hurt him. He could no longer bluff his way through life. Without his hooker money and gone it was; his fun and game.

Louise

Odet Smoked a Joint and I Tried it Too, O.Z. Voorburgwal, Amsterdam 1960s

Hi everyone; I work or stroll, whatever you might name it; I am a hooker, for several years now at my own brothel. And at the moment we have a fun group of girls working here. Three girls also live in the neighborhood. Odette lived on the head of the seawall in a small hotel which also housed many Surinamese men. They moved here from Suriname to become students at the university. Odette met Louis in one of the most famous Surinamese bars at the Nieuwmarkt; the cottonclub. And after a few months they moved in together on that seawall in that small hotel. At first it was all fun and games. Later on Louis made her go crazy, after which she ended up in a brothel. I got along well with Odet. Often we walked around the block when we were working. And that is how I found out that Odet never lighted an ordinary cigarette. But smoked a firm joint of hash. She inhaled so deeply, she almost suffocated as we walked on. So I say to her; Odet what the hell are you doing. That thing smells, put it out; throw that crap away right now. It will kill you. Odet laughed; come on Loes this won't hurt anyone. I can see that, you seem to have difficulty seeing clear; no I don't. It will go away, do you want to try it Loes; stop that you; come on Odet duty calls, we need to get back to the whore house. In the meantime we had reached the binne gasthuis. Odet had finished her joint; smoked it all; and threw it away. Soon we were standing in front of the brothel. And, look at that, we both had customers. We quickly ran inside as if nothing had happened. That night we went our own way. Louis picked Odet up and they left for the seawall together. My sister and I were done as well and both returned home. Odet and I often took a walk in between customers. At times she lighted another joint. Once I tried it; you need to inhale Loes; yes yes. Well let's give it a go. But after the second time; I never tried it again. I wasn't that modern. Lost all control. Everything was spinning; it was frightening really. Not for me. I am stoned enough as it is. And that suits me just fine. For quite some time Odet and Louis lived together in that hotel. Although it never lasted and suddenly Odet was gone. She had met an American soldier and he was stationed at a base in Soesterberg. She called me often while she was there. She told me she was getting married and was pregnant. One time she called me at the Sloestraat and told me he had locked her up. She couldn't leave the house. She panicked. After her call, I phoned the base. The reception, and they went out to check on her. After never having heard from Odet in years she called me; again. She had returned from America with her son Chico and wanted to come visit me. And one day in winter we met. She had brought Chico. She stayed the entire day; we took pictures of each other. I still have a picture of her little son; to remind me of that time. I often think back to those first years that I joined the life. Despite everything there were many good years. I have seen Louis a couple of times as well. For him things did not end so well. He became a drug addict. I guess he did not only smoke one joint once in a while, which is unfortunate. Otherwise he would have lived longer. He is gone now. He started with hope as a student from Suriname. And suddenly it was all gone. There was nothing left for him; not even hope. The great thing is about 1, 5 years ago I met another old friend from the 1960s. Her name is Elleke/ she found us via our publisher Bertram en de Leeuw. She got our address. And then one morning we got a call from Elleke. It was a great surprise. I recognized her voice at once, how is that even possible after all these years. She told me she had bought Meet the Fokkens, tales of the sex room. And immediately recognized them. The guy she is with now loved it as well; they had a good laugh about it. Those good old days. For years Elleke also lived at the Bees. Afterwards she left for America with her husband. After having lived there for years she came back to Holland. We have met her several times in Amsterdam. Went back to the Red Light District; visited bars and had a great time. It is about time we call Elleke again. So we can meet again at the Red Light District for some drinks. To have fun. Bye now.

Louise.

Proposing a New Beginning, Almere 2013

It was a decision; made by someone else. I thought it to be impossible. I believed it to be wrong. From an early age I was taught; but what? This was wrong. I felt for myself; but what? This is too much for me. Where am I; and will I go. He talks and talks. He is a fine talker. And he is sweet talking me in taking a wrong turn. I thought; this is what I want; and it is not something I am doing; for you. Why; what does he want anyway? I thought. Oh my god what am I going to do. Why can't I contradict you, why can't I defend myself; from you. With hate? Oh my god; when will that be. I feel small; and sad. Because all that you are proposing; for your own gain; yes but I; really don't want that. Because for you, you sweet talker, I won't enter the life at the Red Light District. I felt it; you can't do this. I didn't want to. But I was talked into it. I had lost my defenses. And that is how I took the wrong turn. And he got his way. And there I went, after someone else had decided for me. I disappeared and ended up in a window. At the Red Light District. As pretty girl. And I thought to myself; I don't want this, and yet I became a part of it. Because he had sweet talked me into it. And that is how my pimp was born. And I was named; a whore. It was what I had to deal with; for the rest of my life. Yes, it all began when someone else made a choice for me; and his proposition; for my new beginning. Huraa-a-a-y

Louise

The Criminal Investigation Department, Warmoesstraat O.Z. Voorburgwal, Amsterdam

Today was a beautiful fall day. And I had left for work a little early. Because tonight I would have dinner at an Italian restaurant close to the Munt at the Amstel. With my Wimpie. Yesterday Wimpy had come back from a two week vacation in France. And he had brought souvenirs and a strange thin and tight woolen mini dress. He had made me very happy. Thanks Wim. Well, Loes I hope you like it. Yes Wim. The dress is very nice and I will use it for work. Well chosen. Yes Loes, if it makes you enough money we can go to France together. It's a deal. We will see tomorrow Wimpie. How was it at the Côte d'Azur, Wim? Well it was great, couldn't be any better. But Loes I am happy to be back here in my own neighborhood and close to you. Loes, the day after tomorrow the two of us will visit our children. Make sure you have the day off. I will. Well, Wim I am ready to go back to the Oudezijds. Can you take me? I have finished some time ago. Oh well great Loes, let's go! Don't hesitate now. Go on, down the stairs and into the Alpha Romeo. It was just a few miles. After we arrived Wimpie helped me get out of the car, grabbed my bags and brought them to my sex room. Well, Loes I will pick you up tonight at 6:30 so we can go out to dinner just the two of us; bye darling. I changed into my new

French dress and was ready to go; I sat in my window. And before my bum had hit my seat a customer arrived. He asked me if he could stay an hour. Yes of course you can. How much is it madam? An hour will cost you 150 gulden. Okay he said, and paid me. What's you name anyway? My name is Gert, and my name is Marie. Slowly we lay down on the bed and gently I massaged Gert. He became very relaxed. He asked me, say Marie do you have erotic books I can look at. Sure Gert, I have those. I grabbed the books; and Gert loved it. Don't look too long at those Gert, you might ruin the pictures. After he had enough he said; wow Marie these books make me horny. I want to keep looking at these pictures. And then you can wank me. Well Gert, Marie can most certainly do that for you. And then I began to massage Gert from top to bottom. Until I reached the top of his pole; and pulled it in the air; after which he sighed deeply and came. Oh, Gert said, the horny one did it once again. I better be off now. Bye Gert, Bye Marie. Well that was a good start to my evening. Quickly I returned to my throne. At the same time two police officers came by. They literally stormed in; and scared the shit out of me. They commented on my dress, said I had to pull it down over my knees. It was hilarious. It wasn't too short. It was just tight around my body. Nice and tight. They told me that when they returned my dress had to cover my knees. Otherwise we will give you a fine. Understood. All right. Gentlemen. And I thought to myself, why don't you go screw yourselves. What an idiots. I jumped of my sex throne and opened the door, watching the idiots walk away. They disappeared into the alley. Well that was that. Why don't I just stay here at my door. Immediately I saw a customer arrive, waving at me. So it was all good. Why hello Dick, everything all right beneath that fly of yours? Well I am dire need. My gentleman is in dire straits. He is stuck beneath my zipper. Great Dick, I know how to treat that! Well darling why don't you help me with my zipper. Gently open it. Slowly; bit by bit. Dick was tense. Oh, he called out to me; hurry up, open that fly. If you can't open it we will have to use a scissor. As it turned out, I did have to free Dick by cutting his jeans. And there it came bursting out. And we began to fuck standing up. Wonderful darling, this is what one calls, a close call. Luckily I made it. It can make you feel better instantly darling. Well, you said it. By Dick, until the next time. And do put on your sweat pants. I will. Byyyee darling.

Louise

 # His mother's pimp
Koestraat 14 Amsterdam

He became his mother's pimp. At the Koestraat we had our own brothel, and it took quite some time to rebuilt and finish it. Especially because the government and neighbors were against it. Jealous they were. They came up with all sorts of things. But we will discuss this some other time. During our years at the Koestraat there were seven whore houses. Some girls worked from their doors while others strolled around; and another sat in her window. And that is how we met Lettie. She was a great girl with red hair. At first she worked and lived at the Paardekop house, after which she moved next door to work and live. Lettie had been married; and her second husband was a Spaniard. He was a sailor. She had also given birth to his children. And one day he left for Spain. It was hard for Lettie. She even became a drug addict. Those were bad times as her son got involved with drugs as well. However, he wanted to stay close to his mom. Only he couldn't stay at the whorehouse. That's when it happened. Guan started to use as well and he crashed under his mother's bed. The same bed she used when she had customers. It was disgusting. My sister and I tried to help them out. To keep the boy on the right track. Many weekends he spent at our house with our kids. We even took him on our holiday to Spain. However, as much as we tried, it was too late; you could tell when you looked at him. He wanted to, but was too far gone. It was horrible. So at one point he did everything his mom did. He became a pimp, dealer and used his own mother. It was crazy. If Lettie was seeing a customer he would lie underneath her bed. Many pockets have been emptied from under that bed. Many people came back the moment they found out; because someone had taken their belongings. In time Lettie went to rehab. Off she went to the methadone bus. After a while she even sold pills for cash. And Guan kept asking for more money to buy drugs. We just stood by and watched. The landlady also tried to help out Lettie and Guan. And that's when it all became too much. The landlady couldn't tolerate it anymore. They had to go. Lettie moved back east. And there they just continued where they had left off. A couple of months ago I met two of her kids. Great girls, daughters of her Spanish husband. One of them I had already met at my place at the Sloestraat when she was just a toddler. A beautiful child; Lettie had told us she and the Spaniard had 5 children. Well that was more than enough. Three Spanish. One from Lettie's first marriage and one after the Spaniard had already left. And the sad news is that Guan died at a young age. Lettie also died too young. Guan's life must have been horrible. He was never able to do something fun. He was never more than his mother's pimp. From necessity. Never being able to live a free life. Mostly because of his drug abuse. I am sure we will see Lettie's kids again.

Louise

Sheila and her Argentinian Pimp
Koestraat 14. Amsterdam
Sheila and Jordy first sequel

Good morning Loes, are you ready to go. Yes Tien I have everything; clean sheets and tea towels. So let's go. Together we get into the car and head to Amsterdam. Today new people are moving in on the first floor at the Koestraat. Look Tien, we have already reached Amsterdam, through the Wiboutstraat and we arrived at the Kloveniersburgwal. Slow down Loes, there is a spot. Great I see it. We parked and grabbed everything we needed. We walked towards the Koestraat, and up to the first floor, number 14. We checked the apartment and it looked great. Satisfied we looked at each other. And there they were. We opened the door and in came our new tenants. They introduced themselves as Sheila and Jordy. They both came from Argentina. And via Spain they got in contact with Spaniards and Dutch citizens, who knew a way to work at the Red Light District in a brothel. And Sheila started working at the Achterburgwal. At aunt Dien. She also spent some time with a famous boy, called Goldfather Rinus van de Vetjes. The brothel had a good name. And Sheila could start her work tomorrow. She looked forward to it. I said, Sheila do the best you can. She looked fine, with red hair, and she had quite the attitude. Jordy was tall and slim. We left the couple and walked back downstairs to our own brothel. Euchen was already waiting for us with a pot of coffee. Another room we had already rented out to Fatima, a woman from Morocco. She knew what she was doing. And people often came to see her. Fatima do you also want some coffee? I would love some. Together we drank our coffees and chatted, said our goodbyes and went back out on the street. Today many people visited. So we earned our living. We were done for the day. Said goodbye to everyone; and left for Almere. It had been a good day; now let's head to the garden of Amsterdam.

Louise

Sequel 2. Sheila and Jordy Koestraat 14, Amsterdam

Hi everyone. We're back. It has been a couple of weeks since Sheila and Jordy moved in from Spain. And we talk to her occasionally. She likes it here at the Koestraat and at the brothel at the Achterburgwal. Today she invited us over for a barbeque next week. There was enough room for that. The week had flown by and today was the day. There we went, with two bottles of wine, up the stairs; Sheila and Jordy greeted us and we were escorted out back, where the barbeque had already been lit. They filled our glasses and we could get the party started. In total there were six of us. So it was very nice chatting with our hands and feet in Dutch and Spanish. After a while we all burst out in song; the hoogstelied. After we were stuffed and drank enough we left, bye Sheila and Jordy. We closed the doors of our brothel and went home. And life carried on at its usual pace. Suddenly we heard a lot of noise coming from Sheila and Jordy's place, which turned into a horrible fight between the two. And Sheila took off, but now what? There she was, all by herself. So we all walked towards the kitchen. And there we decided that Sheila would stay in the back for some time, until we could find another solution. Sheila was glad it turned out this way. Jordy would look for another place to stay, so Sheila could move back to the first floor. On a certain day Tien and I went up to clean the rooms. Clean the sheets and turn over the matrasses. We cleaned and cleaned. Then we found something under Sheila's bed. A small bag which had contained a stash of money. We counted it and found over 20.000 gulden. Oh I see, it's one of Sheila's bags. She saved a lot of money. Yes Tien, around Christmas she goes home and spends the holidays there. We put the bag away. See you tonight. The room was done so we cleaned ourselves up and returned to the front room. All we had to do was beat the carpets. Come on we each hold a side. One by one we cleaned the mat. At the same time a man came by and took our carpet-beater. Enthusiastically he began to beat the mat. Hey calm down you. All right girls, can I come with you. Of course you can, as long as you pay. The three of us went inside. Put the mat back in the hall way. He was still holding our carpet-beater. Piet we are done beating you know. Yes but I am not. I have got a taste for it now. Well, if that is what you want. Piet paid us and we put the money away. Well, Piet said, now I will spank you senselessly. And he began spanking us with the carpet-beater. At the same time we grabbed him; what the hell. Give us the carpet-beater. Piet fell down on the bed. And there he lay; just right. One by one we spanked Piet. There, Piet, we have done enough. No, he yelled. I can't get enough. Can I stay a little longer? Do you have more money Piet, then we will continue for another fifteen minutes. Yes girls that is fine. Piet paid and kept standing. We grabbed another small carpet-beater and Piet grabbed his john. Together we spanked him. Piet's bum began to glow, he sat down at the edge of the bed, took his condom off and got dressed. He said, thanks girls, I really enjoyed it. At home I will finish what we started here today. Then I will be completely satisfied. Bye girls. Bye Piet. We put the carpet-beaters away and continued our work. The day had almost come to an end. We cleaned up and went home. And there was Sheila, she walked towards the kitchen and we grabbed a drink while we gave her, her money back. She was scared out of her mind. She had completely forgotten about that bag. We had made her very happy. The next day she treated us with cake which was wonderful. She also gave us some flowers. Two weeks later Sheila moved back upstairs. And the peace was restored. We are done for the day. Off to bed; said Tom Thumb.

Louise

 # Four balls yet we peep at the Red Light District

O.O.O; I am excited to walk through the Red Light District to peep at all the beautiful boobies. That is why I visit the Red Light District. O o o I am in the mood to peep. To look at these big warm balls, that is the good thing about the Red Light District. O o o; I am so excited. Yes. Yes. Yes. Now we all peep at the Red Light District; to score; and oh dear, I feel another pair of scorching hot balls in my own pants. And that is how we skip; and sing; together. And that is what happens; at our own Red Light District. And all around us join us in song. That is how it should forever remain; at the Red Light District.

Louise.

Songs in and out of the whore house

Meet us at the whore house, come out of that closet; because life; is one big charade. So if you are in the mood or excited; all of you; meet us at our whore house. Life is still; one big strange charade. Yes, yes; a horny charade. So yes; yes; join us at the Red Light District. Yes, and then we all; score. With the whores of; the Red Light District. All of you jump on bed in the whore; charade. One goes in the closet, and one comes out. Yes-yes that is what is great about this whole whore (???) charade. And there they all go; with their own hip hip hurray. In and out of the whore house they go. And that, my friends, is the moral of this story.

Louise.

Sensation at the brothel O.Z. Voorburgwal Amsterdam, 1960s

Pimp Co; came to learn the truth at the whore house. Today the three of us were busy at work. We drank some tea and talked about life. That is when Jolie told us she had met a nice bloke; a familiar pimp from around the neighborhood. And that they had been meeting in secret for quite some time now. How was he, we asked her. You sure you want to know? Yes of course we are sure, spill it. First of all, he is big and large, with a huge smile and blond curly hair. It was wonderful; having sex together. He is worth the sin. But Jolie, aren't you afraid people will find out. Co won't be too pleased if he hears about this. True, I think he is already a little suspicious, keeps asking me about it. Well, it is all up to you. Come on girls, we need to get back to work. So we walked back to the streets. Jolie had some customers and I was still standing at the door. And then I saw him walking through the streets, Co, Jolie's pimp. Jolie said goodbye to her customer and suddenly Co stormed in. He grabbed Jolie and pulled her towards the front room. He screamed and shouted at her while he punched her in the face. It made her fall to the ground. Afterwards he kicked her a couple of times. It really scared me; started to scream at him to stop, trying to protect her while she was lying on the floor. He yelled at me that he could hurt me too if I didn't stop. I told him he shouldn't try to. That my pimp would come visit him. You better watch out because you won't be able to take his money from him. By giving me a black eye. In the meantime I quickly opened the door. In case witnesses would come by. After a while Co, the boxer calms down. We helped Jolie up. I gave her water for her face. She was unable to speak. I gathered her things. And her bag. And gave them to Co. Leaning on him they both walked home. Later we talked to the Madame. She was not happy. This is not the end of it. Co had to face her after a couple of days. Jolie couldn't go back to work for the rest of the week. But after a couple of days she returned wearing a large pair of sunglasses. She received a lot of customers that day. She had brown eyes, but at that moment her eyes were blue; and all the other colors of the rainbow. How are the two of you doing Jolie, some people at the bar agitated Co. About this new guy I was seeing. They knew nothing for sure. They were all just guessing. They had seen me getting out of some car. Other than that they couldn't tell him anything. But how do you feel? Well, Loes, I know one thing for sure. If I get the chance, I will take off, just me and my blond haired stud. Go someplace far. You are right girl, you should do that. God does that pimp put me off. While I was chatting I met another customer. He made my day. I spanked him with a ruler; spanked him so hard; it broke in two. Then there were two rulers. That is how it ended. And Peetertje was done for the day. Well girls, I'm off. See you tomorrow. Jolie and her blond stud kept their word. We hadn't seen them for years. After a few years we saw them again in the neighborhood. Married. They had two children. A girl and a boy. At first everything was fine. However, the finest pimps end up in the drug world. Because of it they lost all that they loved.

Louise.

To Cut and Shag
Amsterdam Koestraat

Today my old friend came by. He walks in circles through the Red Light District, from store to store. He makes a day out of it. And enjoys it immensely. He knows all the whore houses. Where all my friends are. So today he is part of the gang. He can't seem to get enough of it. And there he was; today, a Saturday afternoon; Diederik walked into the alley. Via the Achterburgwal. There were many customers around, feeling particularly horny. Me and my sister weren't the only two at work that day at the Koestraat. The girls from the other whore houses were also strolling around with their customers. We were making money. Look Marie, its Diederik. Lucky you. Yes Mol, I already saw him enter the ally. And there he was standing in front of me. Looked at me from top to bottom. Shyly he asked me; say Marie. Yes Diederik what's up? Well, I would like to come with you. Okay. I would like to get a haircut and then I would like to shag. That's fine Diederik. You know the way. So go on back. I will be right there. Okay Mol I will see you later. Thanks. So it will be: to cut and shag. Well, Diederick do you want me to use a clipper on your head? Or do you want to cut or shag? Marie I would like to get a haircut first. Okay Diederik, take a seat. I grabbed my scissors and clipper and made his hair wet. Threw a few newspapers on the floor. Towel around his shoulders and there I went. It took some practice. Me and my sister had taken some lessons at the community center. So I tried to remember what I had learned. Diederik loved it. It made him super horny. His dick almost transformed into a stake; I quickly put a condom on it. And while I kept cutting his hair he wanked himself. I took the clippers and shaved his neck and finished. And Diederik yelled. Oh Dear. Now I want to shag you too. And I said, no not today. I grabbed the massage head and put it on his horny cock. And it worked; no shag could top that. Hurraayy. Done for the day. And we did do it together. Hip hurray.

Louise.

To Pay for Love

What is wrong with that? Which fool or idiot; came up with the idea, to create a word for when men go to a woman (whores, prostitutes, or what name one might come up with across the globe). It is madness. To come up with something and create a conspiracy. To hand out fines because someone pays for love. It is the most wonderful and best system there is. As long as everything is dealt with in an honest and proper way. With two people. For the men as well as the women. Abuse or not. Or what the government is making them do; or institutions, or religious people who threaten with hell, if you do something wrong. Well, I can tell you; even in 2014 a lot is still wrong. Especially with people who know nothing, the know-it-alls; who talk in advance. Like a headless chicken. Too stubborn to see what is really going on. Too bad that someone can be so stupid. Stop your pathetic wining and come clean.

Martine & Louise.

 # The Turd
Amsterdam Koestraat

Good afternoon lady. Can I come in? You sound posh. I don't understand. Talk Dutch, won't you; what did you say? How much does it cost? Did the Mrs. give you enough money? Does she talk like you, like she has a turd stuck up her throat? Well, you must be a great couple. Talking from one turd to another, that can't be good. No it's not. That is why I am here. Well, if you give me enough money, I can help you get rid of that turd. Do you what that? To live without your turd? Yes he said, so what's your real name? My name is Pieter. And your wife? Her name is Petronella. Are you serious? And that's is when I started laughing. He laughed as well. Come on Pieter that sounds terrible. Well, he said; I am done with her as well. Yes, for today you must be. Well, Pieter let's get going, come with me to my room; I would love to young lady. And he followed me. Gave me 100 gulden. Great, at least now I am making some money. Pieter washed his hands, put his clothes on the chair and sat down on my bed, asking me for sex books. To look at pictures. Of course Pieter. I grabbed the books and joined him on the bed. He leafed through the pages and his Pete went up in the air. And he said, I want you now. I paid you, so now something has to happen. I want to do everything they do in those pages. Well Pieter, why don't we get started. I don't know which one I want to start with. And he threw the books into a corner. Calm down Pieter, what is going on? And

I took control thinking; let's get this over with. And straight ahead his hungry Pete went in, up and down. And that is how Pieter blew off some steam. Happy and satisfied, with his turd still in place he went home. To his own Petronella. It was his life, which fortunately still meant a lot to him. Bye my darling. Bye, I will think of you. That means a lot to me, so I won't forget you anytime soon; Pietertje

Louise

Abdoel the Regular Amsterdam Koestraat

It is a wonderful day today; in the midst of summer. And off we went, the two of us. Today was Wednesday so we were ready to cut the week in half. My sister was standing at the back door; which was open. Me, Loes, was sitting on my sex throne. In the window. Tonight was a wonderful warm night. The men were peeping at the girls. Look Tien, there comes Abdoel with his circumcised gentleman. Why don't you take him tonight; no Loes, today I am taking it slow. My grandpa is coming to visit. Whatever you want. I will stay here at the door. Come on Tien. Alright, we will see what happen. Too bad, I don't see Abdoel anymore. He always goes for a walk remember. And there he was. Hi, come on in Ab. I jumped of my stool; and almost crushed my sister standing behind the door. Why don't you walk on back? Ab ran through the hall and I followed him. My sister took over my warm stool. And called, do enjoy yourself Loes; I will, bye Tien. I walked into my room, and Ab was ready waiting for me; completely naked. He tried to provoke me, flexing his muscles. And asked me to pinch them. And walked around; showing off his stuff. And I have to admit, he looked amazingly handsome. Massaging his chest I pushed him towards the bed. He threw his pants on the chair in the corner. I grabbed a condom, which made Ab protest. No Loes, I don't want that, I don't want to wear that. You have to stop that Ab.

Stop bitching about this. This is how it works in this place; at the whore house. Okay Loes. But without it; I can spoil you even more; how would you do that? Then I can go on for much longer. With that stupid condom my penis starts to hurt. It made me laugh, the way Ab could come up with new ways each time for not wanting to use a condom. Ab knew what he wanted and grabbed his circumcised john. Placed it in his palm and showed it off. I sat down next to him on the bed. Move over handsome; otherwise we will still be here tomorrow. After that I massaged him from top to bottom. And horny Ab loved it. I took his circumcised Willy; he squirmed and enjoyed every second of it. And at some point his horny john stopped working. And singing Ab left the room. Bye Adboel; my favorite customer. And that's it for today. Bye for now.

Louise

Meeting Someone New and I Could Become a Pimp Amsterdam O.Z. Voorburgwal

My friend Loekie. It was very exciting. Something new and unknown to me. Tonight, my twin sister and I are going out. We will stop working at ten. It was said and done. We had worked; at the whore house. So now we had to hurry, and Martine called; there she is. Are we ready Tien? What do you think? And off we went. Into the car and stepped on the gas towards Rembrandt square. We parked at the Amstel and walked to a pub. We were greeted and sat down at the bar. What will it be ladies? It doesn't matter, as long as it's wet. I agree, the bartender said. So, two small beers then? Sure. Well that tastes great Loes. I agreed and after just a few sips we finished our beers. Well Tien let's get another one. The bartender gave us another beer. Thank you, why don't you take one as well, it is on us; I would love to. And we toasted to society. Say Loes, don't drink too much okay; what do you mean, why don't you mind your own business. No, I mean no harm. It's just that you have to drive. True. We were comfortable. Many people were laughing at the bar. Loes, why don't we go? Whatever you want. We paid the bill, said goodbye to everyone and walked towards the Leidse Square; what do you want to do? Where do you want to go; we'll see. We will go somewhere fun. It's up to you. O; this seems like a fun place. We cross the threshold and are greeted by several ladies. Tien shoved me through the crowds towards the dance floor. Immediately someone pulled me on the floor and into the arms of a woman. And together we danced. While I was dancing I saw Tien talking and sitting at one of the tables. At some point my dance partner left and another one joined me for the next dance. She introduced herself; nice to meet you, my name is Cor. I am Loes; I have never seen you here before. True, this is our first time here. My sister is over there. What is that, am I seeing double? You look so much alike. Yes we are twins. No; yes we really are. Cor stopped dancing and walked towards Tien's table. Hi my name is Cor; you look so much alike. It's wonderful. I would never be able to choose between the two of you. So it would just have to be the both of you. Cor ordered us a beer. So we had enough to keep us going. It was very fun. Tien, I think it is time for us to go. Duty calls, tomorrow morning. Too bad, one more and then we will go. And another lady came over and asked me to dance. She introduced herself as Loekie. She was a blond and tough, sportive girl. Together we danced about fifteen minutes. And at some point I had had enough. Tien was ready to go. Loeki walked us out, asked me for my number and asked if I wanted to go get a cup of coffee in town. Sure, call me. We said goodbye and waved at each other, after which we took off towards the Leidse Street. We roamed through the streets, found the car and went home to the south of Amsterdam. Loes, we had a great time. Yes, we did. That is why we go.

Louise.

We Booked a Hotel at the Geldersekade

Today is today; yes today we will be blunt, we have no money for Christmas. You might think the Fokkens don't need money; they can do everything for free. To eat, sleep, live, be warm; they get everything for free. Forget about it. And today we have been cheated and deceived. Our publisher leaves us with no money so close to the holidays. How are we going to solve that? Well then we will just have to work for our money. Which is, for now, our only financial hope. And there it came, the call that saved the day. Our Christmas customer stepped forward. Great Loes, we have some work. This ain't too bad. Now we can make some money. Do you really want this Loes; to go out this late? It might even be foggy; Tien you know I hate fog, hurry Loes come on. Okay. There we go. Tien, just wait a second, let me go upstairs. I stashed some of our sex clothes up there; in between the antiques. I looked and looked and found the box. Our work clothes, whips, toys for the men, you name it. This stuff is still great; but we can't really use them as they are mouldy. What do we do now? Oh I know, I have a new black lacy outfit. From a while ago. While we were filming with the famous actor Johnny Knoxville. I call Martine; let's use these outfits. Immediately we got dressed. We were ready to go. So there we went, the two of us to the Red Light District in Amsterdam. But this time we went to a sex hotel. We parked our car, and had to get to work. Where is it, Tien? At the Gelderse Kade. Let's go. Yes, here it is. We rang the doorbell. An Asian woman opened the door. Well, I wonder if everything is legal here. We walked upstairs and looked at each other. It was a whole new world. We felt dependent.. and we didn't like it. We had always been our own bosses. We moved up the steep stairs. Here we are. The woman had explained it all. Who the man was; and the payment. We explained her that people always have to pay first. We were ready, walked to another room; and met our customer. He was new to us. And, as a prince, he was lying on the bed waiting for us, completely naked. We put our coats on a chair and got undressed. Not completely of course. We kept our outfits on, and pulled him off the bed. We hugged him and asked for our money, because we needed it for the holidays. We never got any extra money from the government or anyone else for that matter. We had to work until our old age. We were never pampered, so we were eager because this man's money was all we had. He gave us our money; so the games could begin. Tien put away the money, and the three of us danced through the room. We tripped and fell into the bed for an amazing start. He didn't know where to look; our perky boobs greeted him. He touched them with his soft hand, and we were offered a massage. From one to the other. He drifted into a trance and squirmed. He became extremely horny. One he massaged at the top; the other at the bottom. And that is how enjoyed us both. That is how we needed to work; because it would make us extra money. And we had to make do with that money for a while. So we couldn't make him c..me too fast. Suddenly he jumped of the bed. Grabbed his wallet and gave each of us some more money. He asked us to dance; and that is how the three of us waltzed through the room. Afterwards we dove back into bed. And we began our little ritual again. And did he enjoy it; he floated through the room. And then he didn't know what to do; he couldn't chose. Should he pick one or the other? There was no more room for him to choose. He was ready, so with his horny cock he went on top. And there we went, up and down. Suddenly our prince was done, and smirked at us. He couldn't get enough. The prince smoked his cigarette and left the bed. We got dressed; and our time was up. We said goodbye to our temporary prince and went downstairs. We left via the Nieuwe Markt and found our car. Quickly we drove home. We left Amsterdam with both our wallets filled. And if we have no more money we will work again; so until next time.

Louise

Mister S(cr)ewing Threat Met Us at Our Brothel Amsterdam City Centre Koestraat 14

Good afternoon. Hello, mister sewing threat. How are you today? Oh I am just fine young lady. He hesitated in our doorway with a black suitcase in hand. And I kept thinking to myself, what does he want? How can I help you today? Well, I don't mean to be rude. Why? Sir.. Well, why don't you just tell me what you want. Yes, yes madam. How long are you going to stand here? Dry humping me. You need to pay for that as well, you know. I can use some money as well. Well, it is like this madam. I need that other woman who looks so much like you. Oh is that how it is? You could have told me that immediately. I could, but it is nice talking to you. It is such a nice thing to look at, two women who look exactly the same. You are right mister sewing threat. My twin sister has told me about you. So I know about you and what you like. Well, isn't that wonderful. Well, you know what I will go see what my sister is up to. Come on in and wait on the couch. Great. Well, my sister wasn't in the kitchen. So I knocked on her door. Yess? She called and stuck her head out the door, telling me she had company. For how long. Well, it could take a while. I am lucky today. Oh great. Well, Marie, why don't you take mister sewing threat. What does he want exactly, you have told me about him, but now I really want to know. He wants to sew a dress or skirt and then you need to try it on. If it fits the both of you need to stand in front of a mirror. Okay I understand. We'll see. Bye now. Not a skirt made of paper machè right? That's just fine, whatever you want. Maybe I will sew a newspaper together. Sure Marie, now hurry up. I went back to meet the man and there he was. Shall we go, yes I would love to. He gave me his suitcase. I put it on the bed and opened it. It contained all sorts of things. Pieces of cloth and fabric, threat in different colours, and safety pins. I grabbed a piece of fabric with flowers on it. Mister sewing threat paid me. He got undressed. I placed the piece of fabric on the bed. Grabbed the scissors and folded the fabric in two. I cut a piece out the size of his neck. He enjoyed watching me work. Well, young lady why don't you come over here. I put the piece of fabric on over his head. And he loved it. I grabbed a big needle and began to close the dress. O, o, o, my little seamstress; I a love the way you work. I closed one side and started working on the other. Hurry, hurry seamstress. I can feel my john growing quickly. That is good. Quickly he walks to my mirror and stands in front of it. Seamstress, give me a scissor. Otherwise I won't come today. I need to cut. I can do that. Where do you want me to cut? Here why; you need to cut a hole in my dress. Whatever you want. I cut a whole and out it came, his big john. In between the flowery fabric. I grabbed it and put a piece of plastic on it. And just like that we fucked amongst the flowers. And he loved it. Thank you seamstress. He grabbed his suitcase and took off. Bye, say hello to your sister for me. I will. Bye mister sewing threat.

Louise

Drinking a Cup of Coffee with Loeki
Albert Cuyp Amsterdam

Good morning Tien; did you get enough sleep after last night. I sure did, you too? Absolutely. We had a lot of fun; that will keep us going for some time. Absolutely Loes, we can learn from it as well. I wonder if and when Loekie will call. To go get some coffee. I think she will, I will just wait and see. Are we going somewhere today Tien; yes we are, we are going to Albert Cuyp. To get some fruit and vegetables; and some snacks for the kids. Let's have some fun today, on our day of. Tomorrow we can continue our work. Are you almost done? Yes I am. At the same time the phone began to ring. Tien answered. Who is this; oh it's you. Loes it's for you. I took the phone and there she was; it was Loekie. So you waste no time. Hi Loes, when do you have time to meet me. Loekie wanted to meet me as soon as possible. I am so sorry, but today won't work. Tomorrow I can meet you for an hour; oh great. I will see you at two at de Dam close to the palace. See you tomorrow Loekie. Tien do you have enough grocery bags. Yes they are still in the car. Okay let's go. We grabbed our bags from the car and walked towards the Albert Cuyp. The weather was great so we strolled towards the Ferdinand bol; and there we saw the Hema. We walked a little further and stopped in front of the herring stand. It was mouth-watering, so we ordered a herring and ate it on the spot. It tasted wonderful. Satisfied we continued our walk across the market. We didn't miss one stand. There was something for everyone. We walked over to the greengrocer and stocked up. After that we met the man who sold us some oranges. He filled both our bags with vitamins. Generously he gave us one for free. We continued our walk. Bye bye. On our way home, Tien had to stop for a break at the park. After ten minutes we continued our way home to the Ceintuurbaan. We bought some bread; warm buns right from the oven. After that we returned home to the Amstelkade, into the Sloestraat and up the stairs. We took a fresh cup of coffee, and decided to take a break. The rest of the day we took it slow. Tomorrow, we start again. So a new day, with new opportunities. See you tomorrow, all.

Louise

 # Loekie, Amsterdam
Off to the whore house

Good morning Tien; same to you. We need to hurry today. I am meeting Loekie this afternoon. I am curious what will happen. I had already packed my bad. Ate a decent breakfast. So I was ready to go. Left the house, walked down the stairs, and knocked on my sisters' door. She opened and it smelled like coffee. That smells good Tien. Do we drink a cup before we go? Yes of course, the cups are waiting. Do sit down for two minutes Loes. With our cup. We drank our coffees and left. Into the car; to the O.Z. Voorburgwal. We raced through town and every traffic light was green. We drove towards the canal and parked our car right in front of the brothel. We could quickly get started. Fixed the room, and put on the red lights. I sat down at my little sex throne. Wow Loes, you are quick today. Yes I want to make some money before I meet Loekie. Soon I met my first customer; I jumped of my throne and together we walked to my room. After that I had another quickie, after which I left for my date with Loeki. I arrived at the Dam and saw her standing in the distance; waving at me. And there we were; we hugged each other. Great that you came Loes. Okay where should we go? Maybe somewhere near the Warmoestraat. There we can visit a pub. And off we went. We entered the first pub we saw and ordered a beer. Cheers. We had a great time and took a couple more beers. But then I saw the time; it is time for me to go Loekie. It is a shame but I have to leave. Bye everyone; together we left the café and strolled through the streets. Loekie desperately wanted to walk me back to my place, where I worked. So off we went; we walked towards the O.Z. Voorburgwal; and reached my place. I said goodbye to Loekie and promised to call her. I walked inside and opened the curtains. Immediately a customer approached me. Great. Ah my sister is back as well. Well, that took you long enough; Tien. Yes, I am glad I did. What are you doing Loes? Come on let's go home. We left the brothel; and went home. We walked up the stairs at the Sloestraat, and our kids opened the door. Upstairs it smelled like food. Mom had cooked us an amazing dinner. So let's dig in. Say Loes, how was your date? It was great. Loekie will call me for a night out. So I will wait for her call. Now I am off to bed; to get up tomorrow morning feeling healthy and well.

Louise

A Night Out on the Town with Loeki and Loes And I Can Become a Pimp O.Z. Voorburgwal.

Good morning, there we go again. The weeks have gone by so fast lately. We were very busy today. Today my twin sister and I will go out to dinner in town. Afterwards we will grab a nightcap at the pub. At the Leidse Plein, where we will meet Loekie. There we go Tien. Where do you want to eat? What are you in the mood for? Chinese, okay me too. Let's go to the bloemen markt, there we will find a decent restaurant. At the singel. After a wonderful dinner we left the restaurant and walked towards the Leidse Street, where the nightlife was greeting us. That was some great food, right Loes; the Chinese food. Yes it was great. We are almost there Tien. Loekie was waiting for us at the corner of the Leidse Square. We greet each other and walk towards a bar called dancing. We had a great time over there. In the evening we danced and enjoyed ourselves. Satisfied the three of us decided to go home and walked for quite some time. When we came home, our kids were already asleep. The nanny went home. And we took another nightcap. Loekie slept over on our couch, completely in love. Afterwards we met the sandman who made us fall asleep. Until tomorrow. There we are again. I was still sleepy when someone woke me with tea; and a biscuit. It was Loekie, she brought me some breakfast in bed. Thanks, it doesn't get any better than this. Did you get a good night's sleep Loekie? Yes it was fine on the couch, but I would have rather slept next to you Loes. Who knows, maybe next time. My twin sister came upstairs and set the table while I took a shower. I sat down at the table. The children had already joined us. We cracked an egg and had a wonderful time. And then it was time for some coffee. After the coffee I said goodbye to Loekie. Loes, thank you for everything. Okay, see you soon. Call me okay! And she walked down the stairs. I met Loekie quite often after that; had a great time. She was willing to do pretty much everything for me. She was interested in my kids. She had a good idea. She wanted to sit in the red lights for me and give me the money. So I would be able to stay home with my kids. It was sweet and kind of her to offer. I had never experienced anything like it. I am sorry, but that is not something I want. I won't get into it. I always made my own money out on the streets. So I would like to keep it like that. I don't want to be someone else's pimp Loekie. But I want to stay with you Loes. I am sorry but this is where it ends. And that is when Loekie left after a nice weekend. It was sad; but I had to keep going for my kids. I ran into Loeki once and a while; as old friends. Respecting one another. It felt right. And that is how we both went our separate ways. I never forgot about it; because that is also part of this life.

Louise

 # To the Eland Canal Ouwezijds Nanne You Can't Have My Pimp

Good whores don't take it. Solidarity amongst each other. Saturday night; time for coffee. Leen, our Madame came downstairs with coffee and tea. And as it was Saturday a snack. So all of us got cake. Leen chatted with us for a while, after which she went back upstairs. The girls asked; say Loes, how are you and Wimpie? Is he still shagging that girl named Nanne from the Bergstraat? I am not completely sure. It was strange though; last week after work; we went looking for Wimpie. To get something to drink. We went to a bar at the Zeedijk. And what do you now; there he was; with Nanne sitting next to him; drinking. Hi Wim; I thought you wouldn't see her anymore. That you had chosen me and your three kids. For their sake and ours; that we bought that house in Doornspijk at the Veluwe. And then he acts like this. You need to do something like that together. I can't do that on my own. It looked like they were glued to their seats. I had had enough; and said he was done. If you aren't home within an hour at the Ceintuurbaan, I will barricade your door. Just so you know. And that is when we left the bar. Well, he did come home within the hour. He came up with some lame excuse. He was done with Nanne. He apologized. We'll see; how things will end between Wimpie and me. But girls, I don't feel good about this at all. Sneaky little bitch that girl. There has to be more behind it. You, however, always figure it out when it is too late. When the harm has been done. Girls why don't we go out for an hour to visit the Elands canal. Yes they all yelled. She is violating the whore code. You don't run off with one of your colleagues' pimp. It cannot be tolerated. So girls, action; we need to check it out. Tien and I grabbed our cars and we drove off through the Jordaan towards the Marnixstraat, where we parked at the lijnbaans gracht. Martine rang the doorbell and the other girls stayed behind; at a little distance from the house. When someone opened the door, they all joined us at the door. We stormed up the stairs. We could keep moving as all the doors were open. We walked inside, and there he was sitting with Nanne on the couch: Wimpie. She didn't know what to say. Hettie talked to Wimpie; that this wasn't the agreement; to treat me like this; and he just looked at her. Because they were too afraid to say something, the girls became more and more angry. God dammit; come on; Hettie slapped him across the face. I took care of Nanne; and I already owed her the second slap. The other girls helped out as well. And my twin sister said; here take that. Slap-slap-slap from one cheek to the other. What kind of pimp are you. Using two women. And too pathetic to come clean huh punk. Well, that is enough for today girls, this place is dead. Too boring. So we walked back downstairs. To our surprise it had already turned into a brawl right in front of the house as well; and there they came the police with their flashy lights. They jumped out of their cars and were headed our way. So ladies what is going on around here? Well, it's like this. That girl took off with my man. The neighbors also came to see what was happening. One neighbor I already knew said, you all right girl? I have felt better. Is it those two again? Let them self-destruct. They will never work it out. Fight a lot. Girl, your children are worth so much more. Yes I get that. But then you do have to leave me alone and stop being a pimp. Taking my money. I understand honey. We said goodbye to the neighbors and the police let us go. We walked over to our cars and drove off towards the Red Light District, to our whore house. Luckily we were able to make some money afterwards. So Loes, what are you going to do with Wimpie? Dammit I am going on a holiday next month; to see my children. They are going to Spain with their foster family. In Marbella. And their foster parents had invited me as well. And Wimpie had encouraged me to go. Yes-yes. That would give him all the freedom in the world. But of course I am going to visit my kids. Well, girls I am off for the day; tomorrow there is another day. Despite it all; how much fun did we have at Willempie's place. He is always so; strong. Well these days he only smells really strong. What a change I am curious to see what happens. At least he has been warned. To keep his hands off. I gathered my things and went home. I walked up the stairs, put on some good music; and enjoyed some food. I took care of myself and went to bed feeling completely relaxed. I got up the next morning feeling great. Wimpie never showed up that night. In the morning I cleaned the house, took care of myself and drank a good cup of coffee when the doorbell rang. I opened. And who do you think it was? Wimpie; he said; I need to talk to you. And we need to visit the kids together. Oh but I am not going to see them today. First you need to get your act together. Yes, Loes I am so sorry. Yes, well, I heard that one before. Do you want me to drive you to work later? Are you serious; do me a favour. I will find the whore house myself today thank you. Quickly Wimpie put down some fresh buns and squeezed me some orange juice. I grabbed some food and something to drink. Wimpie suggested he would cook that evening. And if I was in the mood for orange filled chicken. That's okay, why don't you set the table? I will be home at six today. Bye. Took the tram to the Dam. On my way I met a regular. He carried my bag. While talking we reached the whore house. My income for that day walked in with me. Fortunately; I immediately made some money. Had a good day today. In time I went back home to the Ceintuurbaan. Ate a great meal. Wimpie was really trying. So that made things a lot better. We made up. And feeling completely in love we went to bed early. So we had enough time to practice. Back and forth; up and down. And that's when we had enough. Completely in love. Until the next time!

Louise

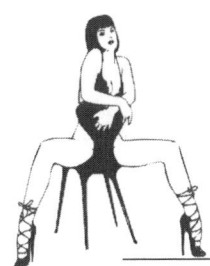 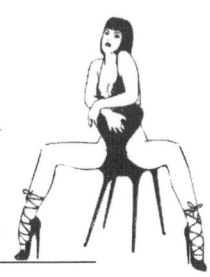

At the Oudezijdsvoorburgwal 97 Amsterdam October 1960s

I had just said goodbye to a customer and was leaning against the door when my neighbor from upstairs walked towards me, screaming and fighting with her pimp from The Hague. He was carrying her high heels and had blood on his head. Hey calm down you two, she punched a hole in my head with her shoe. Yes I can see that, you need to go see a doctor. Yes I will, first I need to take Marie upstairs. Well Marie, you don't look so good yourself. Her pimp told me she had fallen of her stool. Bullshit if you asked me. Shut up you, you want a piece of me also? Because then you're mine. After some fuss he grabs Marie and pushes her up the stairs. Walk you bitch, and soon he punches her a couple more times. Slowly she walks up the stairs, one step at a time. It made sense because she was hammered. And he just keeps yelling at her. You filthy whore. And she yells back, calling him all sorts of things. Marie sits down on the stairs and suddenly he kicks her really hard. She begins to scream and soon my sister came running. Hey stop that will you. The Madame and her husband came over as well and soon the fight was over. After an hour Loes and I return to our rooms. Loes walked back to her customer, who by now would probably have lost his boner. Yes Loes, you will have to work hard this time. Have fun! I go back to my spot against the door and wait for my next customer. Ah the girl from one of the other rooms is walking someone out as well and returns to her spot against the stairs. Well, I had enough fresh air for today, and there comes that ass whole Meier. All he wants is to rub against you. To dry hump against the steps. Well, all right, calm down. At least it will make him come in his own wonderful way. There's no doubt about it.

Martine

 # Amsterdam Ceintuurbaan

Wimpie hung his high work boots with steal noses on the coatrack. What did he want? To quit working all at once, and to continue being a pimp, it wasn't an option. It would send the taxes and police right your way. So most guys decided to work at the Mepal gum factory. For a couple of hours a week they would be covered. Wimpie did the same thing, which worked out fine. However, after a while he had had enough. So he informed about a job as bartender. He loved that. And that is how he ended up at the bar. So Wimpie made it work. Our children were temporarily staying with a foster family. We visited them every week. On their birthdays they would come home to Amsterdam. And during some holidays I would visit my kids. At some point we bought a house at Doornspijk close to Nunspeet in Elburg. The area was wonderful. The kids already went to school there. And there we started a pension with the help of the entire family. It went well. I only worked in the weekends. Because we had made arrangements with Joopie-B. To start a large dancing bar as partners. At the Leidse Square. The kings club. So I did have to work before the remodel. We paid everything together. So that's where all my money went. Everything was going well. So our wish; with our children could come true. Hurray-y-y-y. To provide them with a proper and carefree life. The pension was running well that summer and the kids left for Spain with uncle Jaap and family de Vries. There they had rented two villas for their own family and for their foster kids. So it was one big party. One week later I also went to Spain. When I arrived at the airport I was picked up; by Joke and the kids. It was wonderful. We were all happy. We left the airport and found the place we were staying. The kids guided me in and my skin was so white, I looked like a bottle of milk. Everybody had had a chance to tan. I sat down, drank a glass of sangria and the kids took me to see the second bungalow and my room. It was a wonderful day. I went to bed early. The next day I was woken early by my three kids. We quickly ate something after which we went to the beach. We ran into the ocean. We had a lot of fun with such a big group. Dikkie and his son had come as well. A tall handsome looking blond guy. He and I got along very well. The week flew by and before I knew it, it was time for me to go back to Amsterdam. My kids clung to me; so that was pretty tough. Joke and uncle Jaap took me to the airport. All the kids, aunty Anne, the Dikkies, and many more said goodbye. With a lump in my throat I left; but still very happy. I was ready to go. The plane took off; I was on my way home. Thank you everybody. I am ready to go back to Amsterdam. Back to work.

Louise

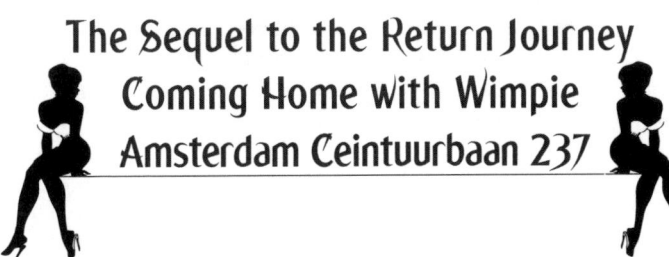

The Sequel to the Return Journey
Coming Home with Wimpie
Amsterdam Ceintuurbaan 237

So, said the KLM. A kiss for you sweet girls. I have put this machine safely on the ground. I am curious if Wimpie is on time to pick me up. Well, quickly through customs and get my suitcase; ah there it is. I grabbed it and left for the exit. And there he was, Wimpie. I was happy to see him. He carried my suitcase. And we walked to the car. On our way to Amsterdam. The two of us. Great, I saw the Ceintuurbaan. Everything looked happy and green. We walked upstairs. Put the suitcase in the corner. We will find that tomorrow. Together we had a nice meal, and after that well I guess you know what happened afterwards. It had already taken too long. Wimpie was getting restless and difficult. He wanted to take off. I asked him, what's the rush? That's when it all came spilling out. He had to see Jopie at the Leidseplein to talk about the remodel for the kingsclub. Well, yes that is important Wim. But I would love to join you sometime. I would like to see how it is going. Where the money I made is being used for. This week we will go together Loes. I thought kiss my ass, fuck you. He quickly took off. I won't be home late he called and ran down the stairs. With a loud bang the front door closed. I relaxed and went to bed on time. Good morning Loes, I made us a nice breakfast. I got out of bed. Sat down and enjoyed it. So, how was it last night with Jopie? I want to know what is going on. It is going along just fine Loes. Well I will see it this week. The bar, yes you will. Oh Loes, I have to tell you something; you do, what do have to say? About what. Immediately I felt something was wrong. But I wasn't quite sure what it was. Wimpie sat down and drank his coffee. He could use a pick-me-up. Spill it Wimpie. And then it came out. Loes, while you were away on vacation I borrowed 20.000 gulden from Jan Tineke. I was shocked; why the hell did you do that? Couldn't it wait? I thought I had invested enough money in that place. Money I made from being a whore and all. I don't know Wim. That wasn't the agreement. Come on. Who is going to have to repay that money? Well, you Loes of course. Yes I will have to. Tomorrow I will talk about it to Jan and my twin sister. Maybe you can cough up some money also? Very funny. Well, I need to go to the Ouwezijdsvoorburgwal. My place is waiting. I will take you Loes. And together we left. Off to the Red Light District. Willem stopped in front of the whore house and I got out of the car. Leen was looking at us from her window on the first floor. Willem stepped on the gas and called, see you tonight. Bye Loes. Yes you too. I do need you; bitch. Loes I am coming down. I walked inside and opened my curtains. I was ready for work. My Madame came in with a tray of goodies and tea. Hi Loes you look hot. How was Spain? It was great, the kids were very happy. Its just, Wimpie is acting strange. Something is up. I wish I knew what it was; maybe he is seeing someone else again. Well, something like that will come out on its own soon enough.

Loes I will keep my eyes and ears open for you; I am going out for a couple of hours. Is it okay if I leave Atax the dog downstairs? Of course Leen, we get along just fine. I continued my work and soon a regular walked in. Today was a good day! Now, let's go home. I have to cook. And there I was, eating alone. And the clock kept ticking and ticking. Still no Wimpie. It was night, but still no Wimpie. What is that bitch up to. He needs to come clean right away. The other day he came clean. Wimpie was seeing Nanne again from the Bergstraat. She saw dollar signs. And had treated Wimpie very well. She thought it was a done deal. Wimpie would start his own business at the Leidse plein with Jopie Boendemaker-Vet. They would open a bar, the Kingsclub. So she would have it all. Just leave Loes to look after the kids. Wimpie will do that. So, that is why he didn't sleep at home for the remainder of the week. He was sleeping at the Elands canal on the first floor. Well, it was fine with me. He could stay away. But don't tell me to pay back the 20.000 gulden. And shove me and my kids aside. I decided he would have to pay back the 20.000 gulden himself to my sister and Jan. Simply walk away, and leave me with the debt? No way. That was not going to happen. So Wimpie would have to be a real pimp now. Well I know what to do. If you don't pay it back yourself you will suffer the consequences as a pimp. I gave him one more chance. Feeling nervous I went to the Elands canal and ran the doorbell. They didn't open the door. Cowards. Wimpie looked through the window. I told him to come down but no one came. I rang the doorbell a couple more times. Kicked and knocked on the door. Told him that if he didn't come down this instance to talk to me I would head over to the police station. To press charges against him. For being a pimp. The police station was across the street. So that would be easy. I walked in with tears on my face. Said I wanted to press charges against my pimp Wimpie. They listened to my story and told me I had to sleep about it. I could come back the next day if I wanted to. They looked in their archive and already had a file with his name and picture on it. Is this him? Yes it is; we know who he is. Good. They offered me something to drink to calm me down, after which I went home. The next day I visited Jan and Tien at the Ostadestraat. I rang the doorbell and had brought my mother. Jan came down, and I began to explain that I would not pay back the 20.000 gulden. And that Willem and Nanne would have to do that. Before I was done explaining Jan hit me against my ear. Which caused it to bleed. My eardrum was torn. So that wasn't good; so I ended up in the emergency room. The other day I spoke to my twin sister. She joined me to see my kids at Nichtevecht. Seeing them made me very happy. Afterwards uncle Jaap, the kids' foster dad came in. He wanted to talk to me so we walked over to the living room. Uncle Jaap had heard that Wimpie took off with Nanne and had borrowed some money. And that he forced me to pay back that money. And that that had hurt me so much I decided to press charges against him. I would never do that if I was with him. I never did. You do understand that do you uncle Jaap? Of course Loes, but I rather you didn't. For the sake of your kids. Otherwise people will look at them and they will think like; you see that, that pimp... let's stay away. Okay uncle Jaap;

but what do I do? Wimpie needs to get his ass over here and we need to sort this out. Okay. That money needs to be paid back as soon as possible. This week, when you visit us again I will make sure you know how we are going to solve this. Great, I better go now. Bye everyone. The week had flown by and my sister and I drove to Nichtevecht to see my kids again. We had a great time together. Uncle Jaap explained what he had arranged at the Zeedijk at his mother's place. Next week. You will hear from me. A week later it was time. At night Martine and I were on our way to the Zeedijk where grandma Vet de Vries lived. Uncle Jaap's mother from Nichtevecht. We parked our car at the Geldersekade. Together we walked to the Zeedijk. Loes I am getting nervous. Tien come on; I have a good feeling about this. If he arranges something; I am sure he will keep his word. Everything will be fine. Okay; say Tien slow down will you. We are perfectly on time. Oh great; we made it. I rang the doorbell and someone opened the door. Can we come upstairs? Of course girls. We shook hands with aunty Mien Vet; and sat down. Uncle Jaap was there as well. We were offered a cup of coffee and talked about everything. About the finances. Willem and Nanne needed to take care of it; to pay back the money. The money they had taken from my sister; the bastards. We looked at each other; it was exciting. Is something going to happen? And yes, Mien got up, grabbed an envelope and gave it to us. We took the cash; counted it and it was all there. We stayed to chat and got ready to leave. Leaving so soon girls? Please stay. Let's toast to a happy ending. Well grandma and uncle Jaap we would rather go home. It doesn't seem like a good idea to walk around with all this money. We are afraid something might happen. We don't want to take any chances. Next time we will all go to the pub. Uncle Jaap walked us out. We walked to the Zeedijk; towards the Gelderse kade. Our dad was waiting for us when we got to the car. Hi girls, did it all go well? Sure dad. Tien got into his car. I said, Tien I am going to go; and walked to my own car. We left for the south of Amsterdam, to the River neighbourhood. We all got out of our cars and walked upstairs where we were welcomed. We grabbed something to drink and toasted to a happy ending. Afterwards we all went our separate ways. And mom and dad left. Bye everyone, until the next time.

Louise en Martine

Koestraat, Jan Sigaar (cigar) 19 Amsterdam

Good morning Koestraat. Well, Tien there we go again. A new day with new opportunities. I am excited Loes, are you? Yes I am. Well let's go then; quickly we enter our own brothel. Our two cats were ready to greet us; Teun and Mies. We petted them and they followed us through the long hallway. To the kitchen. Where we were surprised by cake and coffee. The whole house smelled wonderful. Good morning girls; thank you Eugen. What a surprise. We enjoyed our coffee hour and talked about how everything was going. Everything was fine yesterday, the girls worked hard. They went home at a reasonable hour. That's when I left as well. So let the day begin. Well, the weather is great I tell you that. So Loes and Tien I will head out to buy some groceries for tonight's dinner. Okay, what are you having tonight: Euchen? Well, I was thinking about fried rice; oh lovely; why don't make some extra for us. All right. And off he went with his bags. Let's go Tien, we need to work. Let's see who can score a customer first. We changed into our sexy outfits and stood in the window; tapping it so people would notice us. And there was Jan Sigaar. Hey, do you see what I see? What do you see? It's Jan Sigaar. Oh wonderful. Tien jumped of her stool, opened the door and winked so Jan would come in. Good morning girls. Hi Jan Sigaar. A large cloud of smoke followed him as he walked through the brothel. I closed the curtains and followed them. Jan sat down on the bed. There was a small table right in front of him and he put an ashtray on it. He asked if we had some gin. Tien grabbed a bottle and two glasses. Jan enjoyed it. Why don't you come and enjoy it with me girls. That's fine Jan, but first you have to pay us. Of course. Jan opened his wallet and paid us. We were ready to go. We sipped some gin as well. Jan enjoyed it, saying; gin keeps you healthy. So give me another. We gave Jan a massage and his third leg; shot up. And he called for a new cigar. Tien grabbed another and lighted it. She gave it to Jan. And he said, o-o-o you know how to treat me. He inhaled and released large clouds of smoke. The room was filling up with smoke. I squeezed Tien's arm and playfully I told her, let's go; let's massage this big horny cigar. The smoke turned me on as well. After that Jan Sigaar came while screaming and smoking his cigar. He relaxed and walked to the bathroom. He came back; with of course; his cigar. He left us some small clouds of smoke, drank some more gin and took off. He disappeared to the Achter burgwal. Bye girls.

Louise

Oude Niewstraat 5
Amsterdam 19
Amsterdam City Centre

The – change.

Hurray, today we can make some extra money at a one-man whorehouse. After some coffee; the Fokkens left. Jumped into their car; and drove off. Hit the gas and drove from Almere to Amsterdam. We hoped we would make enough money today. Because only money can put some food on the table. While singing we quickly reached Amsterdam and went to the Singel. You need to get out Tien, I will park the car a few miles down the road. Why don't you go ahead and put the red light on in my room. Okay; Martine left and walked towards the Korjuspoortsteeg. I will see you in a bit Loes. I will make some coffee. Whatever you want. I drove off. There was enough room to park, but it was too expensive. So I drove to the Spaardammerstraat. I found a spot, grabbed my red bike and bags from the trunk, and cycled to our brothel. I made a pit stop at the bakery and bought some bread and some snacks. Afterwards I cycled to the Singel. It was a nice summer's day. Tien was waiting for me at the door talking to a group of men. She scored immediately. The other men walked away while I parked my bike. The other men came to talk me. Hey they said; how is that possible; there are two of you. I laughed and told them it was possible. Let's go, who wants to come first. Me; Peter; called. Well, that is a great start to my day. Great; I could get started right away. My twin sister had taken care of everything and Peter gave me some money. Thank you. Out to have fun today; Peter? Yes we thought we combine it with a work visit. Great. Let's go beautiful girl; Peter was excited. He jumped on the bed while I grabbed a condom and joined him. And massaged him from top to bottom. First I caressed him, then I began to knead him like dough getting ready for the oven. His body began to heat up. His balls turned into to well-done buns. His baguette was 8 inches and ready to go. He yelled you tasty woman get over here. Peter; jumped on top of me. And off he went; up and down; thrusting wildly feeling very horny. Loving every second of it. Soon he was lying on the bed again. Peter looked at his 8 inches. But what was that; it wasn't standing up anymore. Such a shame. Peter looked sad. Yes, well that is how it works with my John. So we wait for a next time. Okay beautiful girl. Bye. Bye Peter. And the men left the ally. Well, Tien that was a great start. Did both of them come with you? Yes, I was very lucky. That's how you make money. And now it's time for some coffee; hurra-a-ay. It was busy out on the streets. It was nice weather for a walk. Tien sat down on her stool and I stood in the doorway enjoying the weather. We were doing fine, a couple times in a row we had customers. I was leaning against the wall out on the streets when the Madame came at us screaming and swearing. Saying, get in now. I was shocked. I looked around me but there was no one but me. So I responded; started to scream at her as well. I asked her what she wanted, do you want me? Come on now. Start fighting with someone else will you. I told you that you cannot stand outside anymore. Oh; who says? The new owner of the houses. Well great, I have been standing outside for a very long time. At Katja's place as well. And at Wies across the street, I see a lot of girls working out on the streets. Well, they don't want it anymore. What is with the arrogance? Say, let me tell you this. It is your whorehouse isn't it? You own the place for years. Oh so as of today I am not? So I am not allowed to move as I please. Stop right there, you can pack your things and leave. Well. Well. You must be under a great deal of pressure. Oh I get it. So the old whores need to make room huh? So; they; can continue their business without restraint. And that is how I was thrown out on the street because of the big money. How ridiculous is that? I grabbed my stuff and threw it in a bag; ready to take off. I yelled all sorts of ugly things to the Madame. And good luck to you. Well, Tien this is just great. Loes just give me the bag, I will see you tonight. Okay, I will hit the streets for a couple of hours; to enjoy myself. Bye; see you later Tien. I walked to the Nieuwe markt. I tried to relax after everything had happened. Well this discussion isn't over just yet. It is too bad. Good; there is still some room at the terrace of the Italian ice parlor Tovani. I ordered a large sorbet with Italian cherries and lots of whipped cream. It tasted great. I sat there for two hours. Met different kinds of people from the Koestraat, talked about the old days. It was fun. I ordered another ice cream. And afterwards it was time to go back to my sister. So I left and returned to the Oude Nieuwstraat. Oh she has a customer. I will just have to wait. I stood at her door and leaned against the wall. Oh; dear I am working out on the streets again. Well, I will see what happens; if someone has something to say about it. I don't give a shit. Ah the door opens and Tien's customer walks out. Quickly I walk inside. Oh there you are

Loes. Yes its me. Martine walked over to her window and tapped the glass. And she scored again. Come on in. How much is it? 50 gulden. Okay great. Tien, I will wait in the back. Girls do you work together as well? I would love to have both of you. Sure, as long as you pay extra. This made Joost laugh out loud. We closed the curtains. Joost paid Martine and we got busy. The dance music was turned up and Joost enjoyed us both. He danced with us through the room. Oh girls I am loving this. You are hot; my horny little one is as hot as a fluorescent tube. Come on girls let's take this over to the bed. Joost lay down in the middle with each of us at his side. He was enjoying himself. One after the other we took hold of his tube. And soon after he came. That was wonderful girls, what a blast. Completely revived Joost jumped to the sink. We began to clean up. Joost left us while he was still singing. See you soon girls. Byye Joosie. Well Tien, I am done for the day. I took my bike and cycled over to the Spaardammerstraat. Good the car is still there. I opened the trunk and put my bike inside. Quickly I drove back to my sister. Great Martine is ready. She got inside and we drove back to Almere. To the Vlevopolder. The radio was on as we talked about what had happened today. Well Tien, I lost my place today. Because of all the governmental bullshit. Know-it-alls. Well, maybe things will get better. Fortunately today was a beautiful day, so soon we will be able to sit in our backyard. Hurray. Soon we entered Almere, took the exit Almere city, to Steedewijk and parked at the Hilversum path. We got out of our car; and saw mom and dad waiting for us outside on the terrace. Hi kids. You can immediately dig in today; we are eating sauerkraut with bacon, a sausage and apple sauce. Oh wonderful. Mom met us with two plates filled with food. We enjoyed it. Afterwards mom and dad went back to Waterwijk. We drank some coffee and then went to our own houses. One at number 4, the other at number 6. We didn't have to travel far because are gardens were adjacent. Bye my sweet Tien; bye my darling Loes. Coffee tomorrow? At your or my place? At both our places? Just the two of us.

Louise en Martine

The Wimp
Koestraat 14 Amsterdam

Tien, we're back. What is up with this heat wave? You took the words out of my mouth. It seems like this summer will never end. One thing we do know for sure. We enjoyed our time at the beach. Cooling down in the ocean. Yes Loes. Why don't you open all the doors and windows here at the brothel, let the air in. Okay, whatever you want. Here sis a milkshake. Out on the streets we sat down on our stools. We loved the warm weather. There were many tourists out today, so let them come. Tomorrow we go back to the beach to cool down again. Hey girls, you look wonderful with that tan. You think? Absolutely, I could eat you up. Zandvoort? Like always. Say Piet how is your chick? Great, I always go out for a walk when the curtains are open. So I always visit my own girl. I love spending money on her. Well bye Piet, go ahead. Enjoy! And do come often; c – o – m – e. Martine took a nice young German man with her to her room. His friend waited for him outside. Throughout the entire neighborhood windows were open. Some of the girls were sitting on their window sills; looking out. They kept themselves busy talking to each other. And then I saw my own little wimp approach me. Don't tell him that. Ah well, he can't help it, that's just the way it is. But still, when he joins me in my room, he will come up with everything to get properly laid. But it still works; after many years of visiting me. I had to get to work.

Hey Janus, come on in. Hi Marie. Isn't your sister around? She is; but she has company. Oh good. The second room Janus. We walked through the lang hallway. Janus leaned against the wall. I wondered what was going on. I looked at him. And my eye caught the enormous bulge in his pants. I was shocked. What has happened to you Janus? Marie, I took some Viagra and I can't get it to go down anymore. I can tell. That's too bad Janus; maybe another time then. And just keep it down, suits you much better. Until the next time. Byee wimp.

Louise

When the Road worker Temporarily Became a Male Ballerina Koestraat

Good evening Tien, are you well rested after your nap? Yes fortunately I am. Sometimes people need some additional sleep. I am as good as new. Great, because our road worker is at the door asking if we are both in today. Oh great; I am ready. Yes Tien me too. He said he would come back in half an hour, he went out for a beer and a sandwich. Well, Loes then I will grab our ballet shoes. Okay, I waited in the doorway. Peeked into the Koestraat; he would be here any moment. And there he was, our tough happy looking road worker. I called Tien, telling her to come on over because he was on his way. The two of us had to be waiting for him; in order for him to come on in, our male ballerina. And there he was. We stepped aside and he walked in; to our room. Hi girls, he threw his bag on the bed and I asked what was inside. Did you buy something fancy? No, I always bring this when I visit you; it is very special. Show us. In a minute. I need to pay you first. Each 150 gulden. Thanks. Is that enough girls? It's fine. He grabbed his bag, turned around and showed us his ballet shoes. Wonderful Tien. And we looked at each other. I whispered, wow they do look fancy and the color red works here. But o.O. they are large and wide. They look like canoes. It took me some effort to keep a straight face. Come on Loes; the performance can really begin now. We put our ballet shoes on. And our ballerina was ready, waiting for us. Okay girls, I will show you how to move so you can join me later. We need to practice in order to perform in public sometime in the future. Great; come on we are ready; so dance dance. The male ballerina danced through the room, head held high, wearing his tutu. We could almost see his naked bum. And underneath his tutu we could see his John grow. So we grabbed our man by the hand. While dancing we guided him to the bed. He surrendered. And yelled, girls I am done dancing. So please do the rest. We performed our magic and he was done. While wearing his ballet shoes he could continue his work as a road worker. Thank you my darling girls. Until the next time. Bye our male ballerina.

Louise

The Man With the Rubber Boots

Ah look who is coming. The man with the rubber boots; let's see if he wants to come in. Or he talks another walk around the Singel. Ah there he is, walking towards me; immediately coming in. How are you Tien? I am fine; now tell me what are we going to do Piet? Today I want to you wear rubber boots as well, and a leather skirt with a red sweater with a deep cut in the front. Do you have that Tien? Of course, let me grab it for you. Put it all on and fill the boots with water before you put them on. Help me would you. How does that feel Tien? It is nice and cool and lathery. Now put your sweater on, it looks great Tien. Just parade through the room, hear it soak and splash from our boots. What a wonderful sound. It is turning Piet on so I fill my boots a little more. Together we walk through the room. You can hear the suction of the water in our rubber boots. Come on Tien a little faster. I am done walking Piet, why don't you give me some extra money then I will keep on walking. Quickly Piet grabbed his wallet and offered me more money. Well thank you, put them in your wet boots. The money sinks to the bottom of my boots, so I stop walking, grab the money and put it in my bra. So it can dry. Okay Tien, stand on my toes and wiggle back and forth. Oh that is so good, I have reached my limit. Grab that stiff pole of yours and wank it hard. A little faster Piet, a little faster.

I am still soaking in my rubber boots and walk through the room. Oh Tien, Oh Tien, Piet closes his eyes and says Oh Tien I am coming. This was great. Piet is ready to go. With his soaking rubber boots he walks out. At the corner he waves at me. Still wearing my rubber boots I walk to the back to hang them out to dry. Afterwards I grab my whorish red heals, and stroll around. Ah someone taps on my room. I open the door. And a young man asks me how much it cost. Come on in, but this story we will save for another time.

Martine

Loes and Tineke. The twins. Guldenwinckelstraat Amsterdam West.

Amsterdam Amstelkade 178. In front of our birth home. Our eldest sister Marijke with her son in the largest stroller. Loes with two children. Carolina and Debora are sitting in the smaller stroller.

Martine with her friend Nellie standing in front of the lampe kappe of Van Briek. The west of Amsterdam, vliegtuig straat.

Amstelkade 178 III. The south of Amsterdam. Mom, dad, Carla, Marietje, Adrie, Henk, Annemarie, Bobbie, Carolina, Deborah, Claudia, Marijke, and Jan. All of us enjoying a meal together during the holidays. 1960s.

Our dad with his five daughters. The west of Amsterdam. We were on our way to the carnival at the Jan van Galenstraat. Marijke, Loes, Tineke, Carla, Saskia. We were all wearing our most beautiful outfits, with handmade coats. Bows in our hair, and real Sunday shoes.

Congrats to the happy couple. 25 years. Mom and Dad Fokkens. Amsterdam.

Loes; and Manollo is flirting with a Brazilian beauty at the South-American bar. At the corner of the warmoesstraat. We danced to the beat, I could keep going for hours. With a sexy dance partner. We enjoyed it everything we visited that bar.

Kloveniersburgwal 18. On the first floor. A one room apartment all-included.

The brothel. Piet and Loes at the Koestraat 14. With Piet the pimp we always had a blast; he was very adventurous. What happened to those good old days?

Loes at the Koestraat 14 in our own brothel, wearing boots, and a sexy dress. For special customers. Never took it off. Please; keep those clothes on.

Koestraat Amsterdam and Kloveniersburgwal 18. Hurray; the Dutch establishment selling coffee and sandwiches has just been opened. They called it 'the two bulls'. Martine dances with Alexander Polo, who was also living at the Koestraat.

Hurray; going out for dinner at a nice Spanish restaurant called 'La Mammie' in Amsterdam. Louise, Noeska, and Martine with a new lover.

Loes and Noeska, my next door neighbor. At the corner of the Koestraat in Amsterdam.

Martine, Noeska, and Loes. In front of the brothel; Koestraat 14, 1970s.

In front of the brothel 1980s. Loes; Koos, and Martine. With our next door neighbor. Amsterdam.

The celebratory opening of the Dutch establishment called 'the two bulls'. Rudo, Noeska, Tien, Alex, Loes. Mom also loves to dance. Kloveniersburgwal 18. Amsterdam.

How about that, Loes with cake. Visiting a friend.

Hurray, there we go again. Completely dressed in leather. From head to toe.

There she goes again? 1980s. In between men. Martine is flirting with the electrician. Hurra-a-a-ay.

The brothel. Koestraat 14, Amsterdam. Loes – Tien, and the French Eliana. She worked with us and lived above the brothel. She was a great girl!

Spanish restaurant. B-Loes. With our Spanish waiter Rafael. Amsterdam.

The grand opening of 'the two bulls'. Filmmaker Jan and his crew from a company called Kruiswijk. Amsterdam.

Amsterdam. Conchita, 6 years old, with Norma a woman from Argentina. A friend of Louise and Martine.

The grand opening of 'the two bulls'. Kloveniersburgwal, Amsterdam. Caro'l, Roeltje, and Arie.

A picture taken in the bedroom. Louise and Martine. Sloestraat III. The south of Amsterdam.

Town-hall, Amsterdam, 1975. Loes and Peppe get married. Their four children are with them. Cousins Arie and Conchita also joined the group.

After the wedding. 1975. A celebration at the Apollo hotel. The south of Amsterdam. Family, friends, and acquaintances.

Koestraat. In front of the brothel, opposite the paper factory. Family Jaring. Loes and Gloria, she came from Argentina.

The grand opening of 'the two bulls'. Loes and Olga, our old next door neighbor. Sloestraat. The south of Amsterdam.

Our poodle Pascha, Esther, Arie sitting in the stroller; and Conchita. Sloestraat 3. The south of Amsterdam.

Amsterdam. Picture taken in 2014.

Louise and Martine. In front of the famous café at the Zeedijk called 't Mandje, owned by Bet van Beeren. Amsterdam.

Zeedijk. In front of the Pop Store. Amsterdam 2014.

O.Z. Voorburgwal. The grand opening of the Red Light museum. 2014.

 # Timid

Timid
She was very timid
And as green as grass.
She was placed in a window
For someone else's joy.
Yes as green as grass
Yes the pimp filled his pockets.
With lots of money.
And she, always so timid.
Was without.
She couldn't do anything about it.
Yes in a window, day in day out, she thought of a better life, oo she was so timid and green.
And yes, she was deflowered in those windows.
Working for someone's money.
She couldn't do anything about it.
She couldn't do anything about it; she remained as timid now as she was back then working at the Red Light District.
And he disappeared daily.
Time and time again; with the money she had made.
And still she remained; timid now as she was back then.

Louise

At the Red Light District

At the Red Light District
That's where you will find them.
The women living in the red lights
Yes; those living in the red lights
We started so young; living in the red lights
Because we thought; we wouldn't be here long.
No longer than two years, do we have to live in the red lights
So we worked and strolled like there was no tomorrow
Tapped the windows and yelled at the customers;
All while living in the red lights.
We made lots of money. And our pimp; he used it for his own good.
That's how it works while you live in the red lights.
Yes the girls living in the red lights.

Louise en Martine

IJmuide, 2011

 # The Red Light

The red light
We are the old whores from Amsterdam
Fifty years ago; we started at the most beautiful place in Amsterdam.
We sat in the red light in the windows.
It was all possible in Amsterdam.
Strolling in your high heels flirting with the men.
That's when they still called out to you. That's when they still knew how to smile. It was all possible in Amsterdam.
You paraded through the Red Light District. With a horny customer; on your arm. It happened time and time again in; our Amsterdam.
We wore sexy dresses.
At the Red Light district,
Is where all the good whores worked.
They knew how it worked. Tapped the windows, strolled through the streets; emptied pockets; and filled them as well. It was all possible in our Amsterdam. To live and let live, to have respect for the girls living in the red lights. That is where we belong. The old whores; of fifty years ago.
From the Red Light District and the inventors of that tiny little red light.
And it all happened; in Amsterdam

Martine & louise Fokkens

Almere, 2013

We Don't Want to Leave You

We don't want to leave you
We don't
What are our mom and dad doing, why?
Where are you, I don't want to leave you.
We don't want to leave you for another family, because we love you so.
Why won't dad look after us?
Why is this happening?
We love you so, our mom and dad.
Mom we cry for you every night, we cry ourselves to sleep. Yes to sleep.
How long is it going to take?
I entered the red light life
Without realizing; what good will that do our kids? I can tell from experience. To a child's life it has no value or meaning.

Martine & louise Fokkens

Almere, 2013

The Old Dog

Do you want to eat first? I am so hungry; glad you are around. I think I am not so hungry anymore. Why Loes what is going on? Tell me; what I am saying is that if I never have sex I don't want to it anymore. Do what; that's when my life ends. What are you saying Nico. Don't be so sad. You are still going strong. Get yourself a sexy broad with two helping hands and a pussy. That's how you have been living your live all this time. Many years you will have in your future, you old dog. Well Niec. Come on, I didn't come over here for nothing. So you can get satisfied. That's how we drank some coffee with apple pie. Niec calmed down. He was himself again. So the games could begin; we walked upstairs. Niec had made his bedroom look real cosy. Well, well Niec that looks very romantic. Thank you. He got undressed. I kept my sexy dress on. Together we sat at the edge of the bed; and he started to massage me. It really turned him on. And his Willy began to grow real fast. He was very happy. Soon I was lying beneath him. And he fucked me good for a while. Unfortunately, his Willy almost collapsed. Niec protested saying it continued to break down. That's okay, let me help you. And while holding his Willy, we rocked back and forth; but it was over. So we relaxed and; I grabbed his cock and wanked him until he came. And Niec felt like he was a young man again. We took a shower and afterwards we strolled down the beach. We bought some stuff for me and I dropped Niecie off at home. Having filled my bags with money and groceries I took off. Niec, feeling extremely happy and content waved at me. Bye girl, I enjoyed it. See you soon, byee. That is how you have to work from time to time. Because no one else will bring you the money; Hurraa-a-a-ay

Louise

Wank the Little Donkey

I am standing in front of the door; and then I move from the door to my stool in my room. I need to find my way, what will today bring, bread with or without ham or cheese. Ah the men are roaming the streets. One walks past my window and yells Hi Ha. Yes; there he goes, the donkey, well I will see him later; that donkey will go roam in the meadow of the Red Light District first. Oh there he is; he walks past me to my room; and waits for me to join him. Hi Ha, Hi Ha, he screams. I say, are you thirsty donkey? Hi Ha, Hi Ha. – I grabbed the donkey something to drink and on all fours he emptied his bowl. Hi ha ha --- nice Hi Ha – the donkey will Hi ha, Hi ha as if his life depends on it. I take the donkey out for a walk in my meadow; my room. My donkey prances of happiness Hi Ha Hi Ha – I hand the donkey its attributes and hold him close on his leash. He grabs his toys. While wanking he comes, and he loves it. He races past me and leaves, prancing through the ally. Byye donkey, I yelled after him.

Louise

Off to the Whorehouse
1970s Ouwenieuwstraat

There we go again. I leave my house, get in my car and head down town. I park my car at the Singel, walk towards the bridge and wait halfway. From a far I can see one of my customers walking in my direction. I lean against the bridge; and see that many men are walking through the neighbourhood. Some nod and look curiously at me. I stroll up and down the bridge and start to become a little impatient. Where is my money? He must have walked across the block. Ah good there he is, my stud. Hi girl are you working here? Yes, can't you tell? Can I come with you? Well Rick, why don't you carry my bag; I would love to. We walked towards the Ouwe Nieuwstraat. My twin sister was also at work and standing in her doorway. We walked to the back where it smelled like fresh coffee. My twin sister gave us a nice cup of coffee and a piece of cake. We enjoyed it. Great girls; I have a wonderful idea. I would really like to have you both. That is possible Rick. You just have to pay for two. Okay, he grabbed his wallet and threw a good amount of money on the bed. Well girls; let's party. We put on some music and the three of us danced through the room. And suddenly Rick yelled; I am in the mood. Oh. In the mood for what? To get laid. And now I want more. Rick grabbed his own hot cock; oh dear who do I take first. It doesn't matter. We looked at each other; and grabbed Rick at his hot cock. The three of us moved through the room while wanking his dick. We ended up in the corner, and kept wanking. Rick called, where am I? What is happening, I am floating. That's okay Rick. Now finish yourself. He went down on his knees. That's when it ended. He c—me happily. Hurra-a-a-ay.

Louise

A Pimp for an Hour
Pimp Dik Was Entranced?
O.Z. Voorburgwal

It was a warm summer's day. I got up early today, I had some trouble sleeping tonight. And when I finally did fall asleep; I woke up because I heard the tram moving across the Ceintuurbaan. Well, all right; let's get out of bed. I shook Wimpie; What's going on? You wanted to go somewhere together right? You wanted to go to the beach at Zandvoort. To parade in the sand. With all your pimp friends from the Red Light District. Immediately Wimpie jumped out of bed. Loes, why don't you get ready then I will make some coffee and something to eat. Well, Wim you are lucky, the sun is out today. It will be a great day. I turned on the radio and opened the doors to our balcony where we had breakfast. Afterwards I grabbed my bag and walked down the stairs. The car was just around the corner at the Amstel. And great, the Alpha Romeo was still there. Wimpie opened the door for me and I got inside. He stepped on the gas as we drove through the Utrechtse straat towards the Oudezijds Voorburgwal, where many people were roaming the streets. Heey Wim, slow down, I see one of my regulars. Where; that blond guy over there. Oh what is up with him? He loves us both, especially you. He loves the fact that you are a pimp, dropping me of at the brothel to make you money. It turns him on. And then he follows me inside; and continues his own game. If you are driving opposite of the canal you can see him looking after you. Until your car is completely out of sight. And then he quickly comes to meet me. Well Wim, I better head in. I saw him lurking from a distance. I got out of the car and walked towards the brothel. Wimpie drove off. Ah and there he was. He threw 200 gulden on the bed which I snatched away. The games were about to begin for Dikkie. He stood in front of me. Well, well my girls, did you work hard for me today? You didn't let others screw you for nothing now did you? Or allow them to underpay you because I won't accept that. I will find those who do. No no, Dik, I work really hard, just for you. You know that right? Yes of course. Dik came closer and forced me to give him my bag and wallet to see if I had earned him enough money. He opened my purse and threw my money on the bed. He counted it all. Well, well, this isn't enough for today. But it is a good start. Oh thank you Dik. I grabbed a condom and took his dicky. I began to massage it. Feeling like a tough guy he told me that when he came to pick me up tonight I'd better have made double the amount of money I had now. Understood; yes Dik. Listen I am your pimp, and nobody else. Sure, whatever you want. Fortunately Dik soon came. With a sigh he sat down on the bed. Wow, that was wonderful. Yes Dik.

We made some money today, you and I. Feeling fit and satisfied Dik left and walked towards the Ouwekerks square. Bye pimp Dik.

Louise

The Carpet Beater Koestaat Amsterdam City Center

It was still nice and quiet at the Koestraat. I had to hurry because you can only beat your carpets before ten in the morning. If you do it a minute later you will receive a fine from the police. And we can't start the day with that. I grabbed one of my carpets and threw it over the stairs; I started beating it with my carpet beater. The thing was filled with dust. Well, of course it was, throughout the day and night people walk on it. I was nice at work when someone came to watch. He said; why don't I give you a hand? Well, I think I can manage just fine; right at that moment the carpet slid off the stairs. The viewer caught it and gave it back to me. Why don't you let me do it? This beating is much too heavy for you. It is, why? I never saw a man beat a carpet before. Just give me the carpet beater; he was completely entranced. I gave him the beater. And he began to beat my carpets. Well this one is done; thank you. Wow this turns me on; I want more; I will follow you in. I want you to give me a proper spanking. With that divine carpet beater. Okay let's go. We walked up the stairs and put the carpet where it belonged. He was waiting for me, holding on to that carpet beater as if his life depended on it. Are you afraid it might run of? No I am not. Okay, so what do you want to do today? I asked; well what I told you a minute ago; okay well that's possible; he gave me the carpet beater. He paid me for an hour; I took his money and started working the carpet beater. He stood in the corner with his hands against the wall. Well, that is provocative. It is time. You need to start, yes I will spank you good; gently I tapped his bum; gradually I spanked him a little harder. The carpet beater went back and forth. Oh this is so good; divine; he yelled. His behind began to shine. So I said; why don't you turn around. He looked like he was very horny. At some point he began to twitch; he even looked a bit like a serpent man. Well, come on, spank my dick. Okay; and that's when I gently began to spank his balls. He grabbed his dick and turned around; with his face in the corner I spanked his bum once again. He twitched while wanking himself and soon he came. Thank you so much, that was amazing. You are very welcome. Bye mister carpet beater.

Lousie en Martine

Pietje and the Schoolteacher
Koestraat 19

Pietje wants to get spanked by Miss pennewip.

Today I went to Amsterdam a little later than usual; from Almere. It was a wonderful late summer's day. It felt great. After fixing my room. I stood in front of my door at the Koestraat. To welcome some customers. There were enough people roaming the streets so I thought; bring them on; I am ready. Several of them asked me how much it cost. Will you help me for free? Why don't you go fuck yourself. Oh and people who claimed they didn't bring any money; but I did bring a watch. I didn't get off to a good start tonight. Ah well, we can't always be so lucky. I think I will get some ice cream around the block at Tafonie's. Good evening Truus, give me one of those big cones, with fruity flavours. And some whipped cream. That way I can lick! Doesn't your sister want anything? No she is out tonight; licking stamps; at the post office. Well, I'd rather lick my ice cream. Bye Truus; good luck making money Loes. Thank you Truus. I will see you tomorrow! While licking my cone I walked back towards the Koestraat. A man began to follow me; all the way to the brothel. I stopped in front of my door. Leaned against the window sill. And then he asked; heey miss can I ask you something? Yes, you especially. He stood in front of me. And he said; I want to get spanked by miss. What do you mean? Well, just. Just what? Well, why don't you come on in. He followed me inside. I closed the door; and walked towards my room. How long do you want to stay; about half an hour. Okay, but you have to pay me first. He gave me some money so we could continue our foreplay. What do you want to do? Explain it to me. Well I like to be punished, to be spanked on your lap. To beat me real good on my bare bum. Well come on then, you little rascal. You always do this, don't you Piet; always looking underneath skirts; they don't want that; do you understand Piet. I don't want you to do that. But miss can I peek under your skirt. No Piet you can't. Well, I will do it anyway miss. At the same time he said it he pulled up my skirt and yelled for me to take off my undies. Pietje stop that will you; I will spank you. Piet! Behave! That's when he threw me on the bed and took my undies. He put them in his pocket. He said; haha miss that is now mine, while he looked at my pussy. Well, well, that is one nice wet pussy you have there miss. That's enough Piet. I grabbed him by his arms and put him over my lap. I will teach you how to behave mister. I spanked him on his bare bum. Until it began to glow. And that's when he wanted to have hot and steaming sex. With the horny miss Pennewip. That's how we all got what we wanted. And it was great. Piet had come. Bye miss.

Louise Fokkens

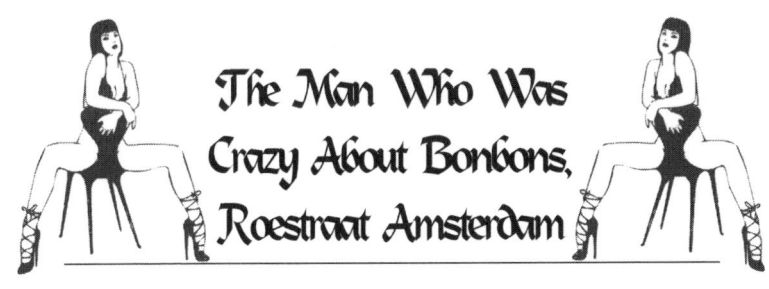

The Man Who Was Crazy About Bonbons, Roestraat Amsterdam

He made his own bonbons. 'Hey, Harrie, how are you doing?' 'And you, Marie?' 'I am fine. Say Harrie, do you still work at your father's cake shop?' Yes, Marie. I still love working there and I make the bonbons myself. I brought a bag for you and for me. I would love to eat them together. I am in the mood for some bonbons.' 'Okay Harrie, I will make some tea.' Harrie put his clothes away and I was wearing a short sexy dress. The tea was ready so we sat down. Harrie grabbed the bonbons and put one in my mouth. 'Wonderful. It makes me hungry for more.' I am in the mood for some bonbons as well,' Harry said. 'Take some, you have an entire bag full of them.' 'Marie will you join me on the bed?' 'I am on my way. I need to move the teapot first..' I lay down and Harrie told me to get some rest after a hard day of work. He put a bonbon in my mouth and told me to eat it very slowly. 'Good.' He grabbed a couple more bonbons and put one on each of my breasts, one on my belly button and one above my pussy. He looked at my body. 'What a unique platter of bonbons, Marie. Beautiful. Nobody has one of those.' One by one Harrie ate the bonbons of my body. When he got to the last one, the one above my pussy, the piece of candy slid down to my pussy. "Well, how do we fix that, Marie?' 'You figure this one out by yourself, but give me another one of those delicious bonbons.' 'I will.' Harrie put the piece of chocolate in my mouth and went down on me to find the bonbon he lost. 'Oh Marie, it just slid down your thighs.' "So what Harrie, just eat it!' 'Yummy. The last one was just as tasty as the first.' 'I told you. So what's next?' 'I will take you between your thighs. What you do want?' Still standing we fucked. Harrie said; 'My bonbons are done. Thank you Marie.' 'Bye!'

Martine

Oudenieuwstraat at Kittie's Place

Pimmetje the runner. A quickie. Kittie was hanging from her window. And said, hello Marie, your tray of food is ready. I am taking my sister out to dinner. It was a Sunday afternoon and spring was on its way; the sun was warm and bright in the sky. I was leaning against the door. Crooked as a whore. Suddenly I saw Pim running at the Lijbaan alley. At that point I knew I had to pay attention; he runs really fast, if I wasn't careful he would run me over. So I was ready to go. There he was. He ran past me and raced inside. He stopped at the sink; and drank some water. Pimmetje was a man of few words. He just stood there. So we had sex standing up; it is possible. To Pim standing up was the way to go; this is great he yelled. I asked Pim if he was going to do something nice that day. Yes Marie. I am going to Artis this afternoon. Oh to meet your family. Yes, Marie, why don't you come with me? Nah Pim, that family of monkey's is sick of me. For now. Well, Marie, I need to hurry. I will see you next time! Quickly Pim left.

Louise

The Shopping Mall
Jantje Fish IJmijden July 2011

On a Friday morning I went out for some groceries at the shopping mall called Zeewijk. With my twinsister. My sister visited a supermarket; to buy a bottle of blood wine. When I came back from the wine store I saw a group of men sitting at the red bench around a stone pillar. I walked over to them and they greeted me. They were awfully jolly. Heey girl, how are you today? Me? What do you think? Can't you tell? Fit as a fiddle and always ready to go. I sure hope you feel the same. The men started to laugh. Jantje my regular was sitting amongst them. And said; Marie I often cycle by your house. To see if I can catch a glimpse of you. Well, that is allowed. Yes I always want to come in for some coffee. You should! But do bring a nice piece of cake. Otherwise I won't let you in. Suddenly another chimed in by saying; Jan your wife is coming over here. Be careful. Aren't we allowed to talk, I asked. Act normal will you. She is no different from me, and I do not intent to run away from her. Suddenly I don't count anymore? You look like obedient little puppies. And there she was. I said, good afternoon, how are you doing? She looked a little surprised. I got a little fed up. If I was a guy I would run from a scarecrow like her. She was what all the men were afraid of? Why? They all want to have fun. Well I've had enough for one day. Fortunately my sister was done shopping and joined me. Hi, did you get everything you need? That took you long enough. Yes, I'm sorry. Come on; let's go find our car; we had to hurry. Because we were meeting someone in Amsterdam. On our way I talked about that woman I met a couple of hours ago; at Zijwijk. I had known Jan from the sixties with his beautiful blond head. We always had a good laugh. What is that about; I had been living in Ijmuiden for over a year now and all of a sudden I meet one regular after the other. Jan fish is one of those regulars. That's how I always used to call him. When he came over to fuck he always brought me some fish. From the fish market. It was great. At home everyone would join in on the meal. One day I ran into Jantje fish again; he almost hit me with his bike; he stopped and asked me what I was doing here. I wondered the same thing about him. It has been years; you are right about that! How are we, I asked? Jantje laughed and gave me a horny look through those beautiful blue eyes of his. He thought it was nice to meet me that day. Which was obvious since he asked me where I lived. Nearby; where! There! In one of those flats. Oh so I did get it right. Say Marie, can't we go do something together. Why. Well, like the old days, when you were still working at the red light district. When I came to see you. Those were some wonderful times. Yes it really was fun, too bad it's over. It was a lot more fun back then, much safer as well. Well, those days are gone. That's why I don't go there anymore Marie. Can I come over again, I will bring some fish. I can do that right? Why just for fish? If I would? You would need to some money to finalize that deal; a lot of it. Are you for real?

Come on Jan, it will cost you more if you book a private session! You can't just come over and pay me next to nothing to get a full treatment; I don't care how horny you are. Then do it yourself! With those giant hands of yours. Nice and cheap. Safe you some money. Well Jantje fish I am off. Duty calls. I walked towards my house. Looked back one more time. With a sad look on his face Jan was watching me walk away. I waved one more time; and called, well that's just too bad. Bye Jantje fish; perhaps we can relive those old days another time. Byee.

Louise

The Great Wobbler
Amsterdam Koestraat

Good day everyone! This week has gone by too fast. Today it was Monday. A new start of the week. I wonder what this week will bring. Hurry up Loes. All preperations have been made; for tonight. So we better relax. I grabbed my bags and went to the Red Light District. I grabbed Line 25. It was a warm day, but it rained as well. The tram raced through town and before I knew it I had to get out at the Dam. We could get the party started. I ran into some of my friends on my way in. We chatted and afterwards I went to work. I could walk right in because today the brothel had been cleaned from top to bottom. Our aunt, a sister of our mom, always cleaned our place. She lived in Schaage and had left Amsterdam for quite some time. So she loved going back to Amsterdam once in a while. The other girls working at the brothel got along with our aunt just fine. So I immediately walked out back to the kitchen to get some coffee and a biscuit. This is great auntie; you want another cup Loes? I would love to, but first I need to get changed. I walked towards my room and put a sexy dress on. I felt great. I got another cup of coffee and drank it immediately. Afterwards I left for my throne. I opened the door, and the show could begin! I stuck my head out the door. And guess who I saw shuffling through the alley. Hey that's the wobbler! I yelled for him and he turned around. With his enormous boots he ran through the alley and grabbed me, lifted me up in the air and put me down in my room. It was hilarious. With Wiebe everything went fast. He gave me some money. I quickly grabbed a condom, and shoved it on his penis. Gracefully Wiebe jumped on top of me. And he wobbled back and forth. And up and down. But the wobbling was his favourite part. He never wanted or asked for more. Wobbling and wobbling my wobbler became very horny and came very soon. He fell down next to me and said, well Loes were done! I am once again a winner. And your biggest wobbler. Yes Wiebe that's true, well, congratulations. It was great. Before I knew it Wiebe had taken off. I ran after him and closed the door behind him. I heard him say goodbye; lots of love from je biggest wobbler. That was that. A perfect start to a great day. Quickly grabbed another cup of coffee. Lots of love my old wobbler.

Louise

 We Go Out Clubbing and Get Some Extra Attention From a Woman.
Amsterdam O.Z. Voorburgwal

Oh what's that? What the hell? How did that happen? During this period I danced through my life. It's what saved me. All the men; to whom I had always been sincere had left me. They left me because of greed and short-sightedness; left their own blood, their children alone. Their lives were just too damn good. And because of it; didn't know how to continue their lives. Just didn't understand it anymore; their wonderful lives. They continued their lives together. They wanted their lives to be even better, so they just gave up on the one they had. Ice cold; like a thief in the night; they took off. Leaving me, my worries, and my fatherless family behind. I recovered my strength and continued my life. I became a mom and a dad. Regained my strength for a long time. That's how I continued my life; the way I always did. I continued my work at the Red Light District. To earn a living for my kids. Because my exes; they could only take care of themselves. They had this pimp mentality; all they thought about was themselves. Taking care of their kids; they didn't have time for that. So one night of fun was something I could really use. So, today, on Saturday, after a couple hours of work it was time for me and my friend Selma to go clubbing. Where do you want to go first Loes? Well, what are you in the mood for Sel? Well, why don't we go to the Amstelstraat first. And afterwards we can get a night cap at the Leidse Square. There is also the Dansing, which is open at night. Okay. We got into the car and drove to the Amstel where we parked the car. We walked towards the Paardestraat. The music met us when we walked into a bar where we were greeted by a lot of women. We were immediately offered a stool. We sat down. Are you comfortable Selma; I am. But Sel, we won't find a man out here. Shouldn't we go somewhere else? Of course not Loes. We see enough guys as it is, at the Red Light District. That is true. Come on girl, relax. Take a sip. The bartender offered me some gin. Selma took a small beer. We started talking to some tough looking women. Life started to look a lot better, so we took another drink. A nice tune was playing. So one of those tough looking women pulled me towards the dance floor. We danced together, through the bar. I was feeling great. Tea brought me back to the bar and put me back on my seat. It made me laugh. I loved the attention. Tea never left my side. She wanted to know everything about me. Selma was having fun as well. She was talking to some people she knew. Hey Selma, you really do know everyone don't you. Yes Loes, but I come here often. Oh okay. I had fun Sel, but why don't we go have a drink a few miles down the block. I paid for our drinks and Tea asked me if she could call me; I gave her my number. I said goodbye to everyone we met and we left the bar. Strolled to the corner at the Amstel. We went to the Amstel tavern.

Selma walked inside and greeted everyone she knew. Hi girls, how are you all doing? What do you think, we are doing great. We had a great time and Selma had had plenty to drink. Why don't you drink some more Loes? Come on; I have been drinking enough. I am better driver when I drink a soda. You see. Oh that's right. The night ended too soon. Come on Sel, i've had enough, let's pay for our drinks and leave. We left and bought a sandwich on our way to the car. It tasted great. I dropped Selma off at her house and raced towards the south of Amsterdam. Great there is still room to park my car. When I came home I made some tea and took a shower. For today everything was fine. I had enjoyed this new experience with all these tough women. We never got to visit the Leise Square but we will go there some other time. That's it for today. Lots of love, and until the next time! Hurra-a-a-ay

Louise

My Pimp Was Having the Time of his Life Amsterdam 1960s O.Z. Voorburgwal

I am done working for today. Saturday is over so I was on my way home. It was a warm summer's day. And a nice evening to walk home. Bye girls. I left the O.Z. Voorburgwal and walked through the oude Hoogstraat after which I strolled towards Rembrands square. On my way home I bought a sandwich. Soon two men began to follow me. One yelled at me and the other tried to get me to come over by saying psst-psst. Can I ask you something? I looked at him and said; you can always ask me something. What's up. Well, I have been watching you for quite some time now. Oh? Yes, I mean you work at the Ouwezijds right? Yes that's true. I wanted to come to you tonight; but unfortunately you just left; the brothel. It was bad luck. Yes it really was. So what now? Say beautiful woman, can't we booked a hotel, just the two of us. I will pay you lots of money. I have been longing for you for so long. I had made enough money today, so I didn't have to make more. I looked at him; this farmer's boy from Drenthe. He looked decent and trustworthy. So I said, okay Gijs let's do it. Let's see if they have a room for us at the Amstel. We walked around the block and walked towards a hotel. The night manager greeted us. Good day how can I help you guys. We would like a room. That's possible. We wrote ourselves down as a couple. We paid and got the keys to the room; two towels and some soap. We walked upstairs. The place was a mess. I didn't like it; Gijs looked like he wasn't too comfortable either. Well, let's just get this over with, I thought. The sooner we can leave this place the better. Gijs paid me and I knew just what to do with the money. We jumped in bed because the game of love had to be played. Gijs was a real man in bed. Soon we finished and satisfied we jumped out of bed. We cleaned ourselves up and left. Soon we were out on the streets. He gave me a kiss goodbye and we both went in opposite directions. I walked and before I knew it I was at home. I opened the door and suddenly I saw Willempie waiting for me. Hey where have you been Loes? I was at the whorehouse; to pick you up; thought we might go out or something. Just the two of us. Well, that is too bad. It was a nice warm summer's night; so I thought to myself I would stroll home. So I was busy. What are we going to do tomorrow Wimpie? Do you know? Absolutely, we are going to the beach. To cool down in the ocean. Wonderful Wimpie. Hurraa-a-a-a-ay

Louise

The Brothel
1972 O.Z.

Who will take care of my kids? After haven't worked for quite some time leaving us with almost nothing to spend, my kids were fed up. After the birth of my fourth child; a girl in September 1971. The father of my three oldest kids and the father of the youngest never paid a dime; for their own blood. You will never find better pimps. Their life existed of taking money from others. Even at the expense of their own children. They never even tried. So on a Monday afternoon I took a chance. I walked towards the Red Light District. There I met Harrijet at the O.Z. Voorburgwal. I rang the doorbell; and after a couple of more tries Harrijet opened the window; who is it she yelled. Oh it's you, the twins. I am sorry she said but in the afternoon I always take a nap. Because I work through the night. Oh that's okay Harrijet. What brings you here girls? I wanted to ask you something. Okay come on up. I will open the door. With a bang the door opened. A high voice yelled for us to come in. We walked through the narrow hallway and up the stairs; to the first floor. Hi girls, sit down. We sat down. What do you want? Well, I am looking for a place to work for two or three nights a week. Say Loes, how are things with your youngest, the one you had with the Spaniard. She's great. But the idiot won't pay me. So I am forced to make some money for myself. Because that's how it works. Would you like some coffee girls? We would love some. We drank our coffee and ate a biscuit. At the same time we admired Harrijet's cats. She had about 20 of them. The place smelled like cat as well. One jumped on my lap. Well Loes I have two free nights during the weekend. If you want you can start the day after tomorrow. I would love to. What room is available? The middle room, it is the smallest one here. Oh my god, I thought; I hope not. Say Harrijet you won't force me to work on the toilet right? Ah what the hell. I have a place to stay. We drank another cup of coffee and said goodbye. Okay Tien, first we need to visit Meijer for a pair of high heels. Can you lend me some money? Of course, Tien said. If I can make you happy with some new shoes, I will buy them as a gift. We walked towards the stores, bought some new shoes. How are they Loes; they are great Tien. Let's get something to eat at the bakery. Afterwards we quickly walked to the car. We need to hurry Tien, the kids will be home from school any minute now. We got inside and drove home. Having arrived home we made some tea and there they were. The kids stormed in and told us about their day. Well, that's it for today. The day after tomorrow

I will go back to work at the Red Light District. To make some extra money. We really need it.

Louise

 # Back to Work O.Z. Harrijet 1972

I got into my car and drove off; to Harrijet. Back to work, in the smallest room at the brothel. Probably the smallest room at the Red Light District as well. I was fine, I would just have to improvise. Finally, I am here. I was lucky as I immediately found a spot to park my car. I parked my car, hopped out and saw Harrijet hanging from her window. Hi Loes. I am coming down. She offered me a key to the whore house. We talked a little before Harrijet went back upstairs. I walked down the hall to the second room. I opened the door and almost tripped over the bed. There was hardly any room to walk around. It was hilarious. Well come on Loes, let's get dressed. I stood in front of my door. Said hello to one of my colleagues and looked for customers. Soon a group of young men walked towards us. Hi guys, are you ready to come in? Sure, how much does it cost? 50 gulden. Great. He walked in with me. Nelus walked in with my neighbour. So she closed her curtains. We walked through the hallway and there we were. Put your clothes on the chair. We barely had room to move around. I felt a little embarrassed. I hadn't worked for quite some time after the birth of my fourth. And because of the size of that room. Well, let's just get this party started I thought. So I began to talk to Peter, and danced with him through the small room. I sweet talked Peter into heaven. Asked him to please stay an hour. He immediately gave me 150 gulden. So that was a great start of my first day. I was very lucky. We shuffled towards the bed and fell down. I put on some music and Abba started playing. Fucking me Peeter tried to please me. First on top, then on the bottom; with that though looking man. After that there was no stopping it, with one firm thrust Peeter reached his happy ending. Satisfied he lay down beside me. Until he came back to reality. Gracefully he jumped of the bed and before I knew it he was fully dressed. We left the small room and walked back to the streets. His friends were waiting for him at the bridge. And immediately asked him how it had been. Did you get her good? Yes I sure did, it was wonderful. The guys said goodbye and left. Wow that was a great start to my evening. I hope to get two more customers before I can go home. Harrijet met me with some coffee. We talked for a while before I went back to work. Around one at night I had had enough. With a purse filled with money I went home. Bye Harrijet I will see you tomorrow.

Louise

Stoned as a Shrimp +- 65 O.Z. Voorburgwal Amsterdam Sloestraat

Good morning everyone! Loes we need to hurry. As an arrow I shot through my house so I would be able to leave quickly. Everything was tidy. I drove to the O.Z. Voorburgwal, to my brothel. I got ready and put the red light on. Let's get the party started. I opened my door and could hear the church bells at the Ouwekerksplein. Soon I saw a couple of curious men walking by. Some asked me how much it cost. Well why don't you come on in first; or are you afraid? He left. Before I knew it Joeri raced inside. He was one my regulars. I knew exactly what would happen. So that was great. Joeri put some money on my cupboard. Afterwards we danced through the room. Suddenly we tripped and fell on the bed. Joeri kept saying how beautiful I was and how much he enjoyed being with me. He entered his own seventh heaven. With a loud cry he said he regretted nothing. Loes this was great. Now I better go. Otherwise I might come again. Okay Joerie; until the next time. I cleaned up the room and soon it looked as if nothing had happened. Who's next? I walked back outside and looked out. Soon I saw Oeri boeri walk towards me. Before he walked in I grabbed something to drink. When I came back out he was standing right in front of me. He looked at me with those dark brown bedroom eyes; I thought to myself, be careful Loes. Don't fall for his tricks. Well, we will see what happens. He was a stud and very nice to look at, with his skin the colour of coffee. And in the sack he was wonderful as well. My bed was close. He paid and I put the money away. Let's get this party started. I thought to myself, Loes you need to keep control; take care of this guy. We shared the bed and massaged each other. Soon I felt Oeri Boeri reach his limits. He jumped of the bed and said it all went to fast. Loes I don't want to come just yet. I need to keep going. So I will smoke another cigarette. Whatever you want; Oeri Boeri lit his cigarette and soon the room was filled with smoke. Looking at me he offered me his cigarette. Well, all right. It tasted funny. Say Boeri, what is this strange taste. I could get really sick from this. You will be fine Loes. I'd better be. I gave him his cigarette back and he put it out. We continued where we had left off. Boeri was doing a great job. Soon the fuck was over, we were both satisfied and had really enjoyed it. Loes, I need to hurry I am almost late again. So I will go now. Okay, it was strange that he asked me how I was doing. Are you feeling all right? I am fine. Well Loes, I will see you soon. I walked back to my room and cleaned up. Afterwards I walked back to my throne in the window. The church bells were ringing and played a joyful tune. It was crowded on the streets. There were enough potential customers. So bring them on. I was comfortably sitting on my stool when all of a sudden something strange happened to my head. I was banged on the head and saw flashes of light and even some stars. To make matters worse the church bells began to ring even louder. I got a little scared and worried. Fortunately I saw my sister approaching. She let out one of her customers.

Hey what's up with you. You look horrible. Tien I am seeing double and it is getting risky. Okay get dressed we will go see a doctor. My twin sister helped me up and together we walked to the doctor. Fortunately he was at home. We were invited in. I told him the entire story. What was wrong with me and that I had this customer who offered me his cigarette. Which might have caused this whole thing. I think you are right, he said. He looked into my eyes and checked my blood pressure. Fortunately it all looked fine. What do I need to do now doctor? You need to eat something and get something to drink. And take a couple hours of rest. Then the feeling will go away and everything will get back to normal. Okay, thank you doctor. And don't smoke any of those strange cigarettes. You can't handle those. So don't let anyone force you to smoke them. It can be dangerous. I won't, thank you doctor. If in an hour you still feel the same come back to see me. Thank you. Afterwards we walked back to the Voorburgwal, to the brothel. Tien put me to bed and told me to get some sleep. I will come check on you every fifteen minutes or just call for me. I will keep on working. Quickly I fell asleep and soon I felt a lot better. I was so happy. Soon my twin sister came to check on me. How are you? Oh I feel great. But Oeri Boeri won't get away with this again. Is he crazy, he can't do this. For another ten minutes I stayed put and afterwards I cleaned myself up. I went back to work for another hour. Welcomed two customers. Afterwards the two of us took off, ate a sandwich and drove back to the south of Amsterdam. We had fun that night, so despite everything that had happened we still had a great day. Satisfied we went to bed. The next morning we woke up feeling great and not stoned as a shrimp. I never wanted to feel like that again.

Louise

My Jatmous
I Can't Turn Him Down
O.Z. Voorburgwal Amsterdam 1963

There we go again. Today; Monday, so a new week, with new chances. I was feeling great. And was very active; so soon I was standing in front of my door ready for customers. Let those men come. There were a lot of men roaming the streets. Lots of seed carriers. Soon a customer came cycling towards me. He stopped, jumped of his bike, threw it against a tree and ran towards me. It looked like he was in dire need. And he definitely was. Hey girl; can you wank me; of course you always. He walked towards my room and looked at me. He said, my sweet sweet girl I only have 10 gulden. Well look again, you sure you don't have more? No unfortunately I don't. And I haven't gotten any for over a week. Oh dear that is long. Well, all right come on back. Watch your step. I didn't want to give up a perfectly good customer. He was bound to bring me luck. Guus paid me and I quickly put it away. Soon he was wanking himself and admired himself in the mirror. Look at me; with my big dick. Girl help me out would you. I wanked him hard and soon he came; Guus thanked me. I am done for today. Quickly he took off; jumped on his bike. He called out for me. And disappeared. Quickly I cleaned my room. And now

I needed to wait for the next customer; maybe I will be lucky?

Louise

The Fucker
Amsterdam Koestraat 1975

He was a great fucker. Today was a wonderful warm summer's night. The neighbors were hanging from their windows or were sitting outside. The terrace at the corner close to the Italian ice parlor was full; with people eating their ice cream cones. My sister and I got some ice cream as well and were enjoying it. We talked to our neighbor and soon I saw mister fucker come closer. He was this tough looking blond guy. Hi Marie; Hi Toon. Marie, which room will we use this time; the front or the back? Today; the third room. Okay, he walked towards the room and put the money on the sink. I counted it and put it away. Toon showed off his body as he walked through the room. You look great Toon. He loved it when I gave him compliments. That he looked very handsome. And had a very sexy body. Get ready Marie, I thought. It is time to work. Toon got ready as well, stretched and flexed his muscles. Looking very tough he approached me. He lifted me of the ground and before I knew it I was lying in his arms on the bed. Let's get this party started. Toon was an amazing fucker. He fucked as if his life depended on it. And I knew my way around as well, and loved it. So soon we both reached our happy ending. We were very happy; and satisfied. Toon stayed for a while. We drank a cup of coffee and afterwards he walked away and left the brothel. Bye my sweet Marie. Soon I will be back.

Louise

Meringue
Ouwe Nieuwstraat Chrissie

I got off to a great start today. Ah I see Barend Bluf coming over. His cock forward; he was always bragging about it. It was everything he had left from his business. Always bluffing, slightly arrogant; he told me he was amazing in bed. With his giant cock; with which he could get any woman he wanted. But after years of in and out; Crissie had some difficulties in the sack. He couldn't keep it up anymore. It was very depressing for him. His world fell apart. He saw no reason to live anymore. However, here he was. He walked in and lay down on the bed. Hi Crissie, what's this? Worked hard; yes Loes that too. But it's not just that. Tell me, what is going on? Wait I will pay you first. Yes please. Here you go; thank you. I sat down at the edge of the bed and caressed his hair. At the same time he told me that his John refused to work these days. I looked at him. And he was right, his amazing giant cock was nowhere to be found. What was left was something which looked like a small piece of meringue. Well, Chrissie it just means we have to work a little harder. I immediately got to work. I massaged his John. Oh; wonderful Cris said, it is working. Well, that's what it's all about isn't it. Just wait and see Cris, I am sure it's only temporary. And hey small penises get what they want as well. He laughed. Yes Crissie, as we get older; everything changes; even the sex. It's great, a new phase in your life. At least you don't have to brag about your dick anymore. That's true. It was exhausting at times you know. Well, Loes I am off. Okay; Crissie, and don't forget to practice. Practice what? Well you know, this massaging technique. Similar to how I just massaged you. So have fun with that little meringue of yours. I will. Thank you. Bye Loes.

Louise

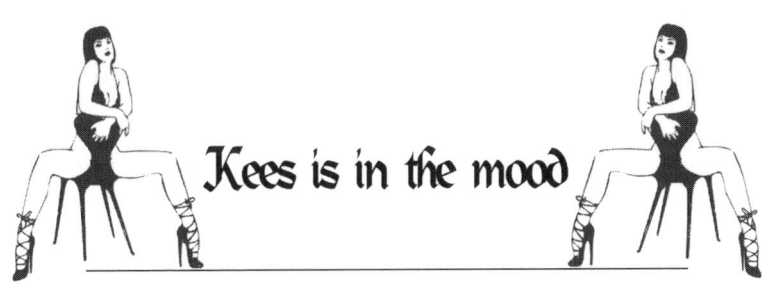

Kees is in the mood

Hi everyone. Today the weather was great, a nice day in spring. One of those days where you need to get out. Which is what I am going to do today. Hopefully I will meet some nice customers today. I was standing in my doorway and saw enough men looking for love. For a girl who knows how to have fun. Soon I notice a stud; and looked at him from head to toe. He is wearing a tight suit looking beautiful. The girls from across the street notice him as well. Suddenly he walks over to meet me. I am curious what will happen next. He looks at me. Damn girl you are hot. Why? Well, you look good enough to eat. Oh is it that bad. I want to come with you. Now I knew I had to be careful. That's 50 gulden. Okay for you. Oh thank you. He walked inside and I closed the door. He immediately paid me. He hugged me and was ready to go. Wow you are so beautiful and sweet. I am loving you. You are an amazing woman. All right, that great. You are nice as well.

Immediately he threw his clothes on the chair. Butt naked he strolled through the room, showing off his body. Suddenly he lifted me up in the air.

Oh I am holding such a hot woman. Say Kees, this isn't a circus show you know. I know, but don't you feel how strong and powerful I am. You sure are. Why don't you show your strength at a gym. Put me back down, one pimp is enough. Now let's get this thing over with. Finally Kees is done showing off and lies down on the bed. Soon he calls me; come on over here hottie. I will royally fuck you. Afterwards you will never want anyone ever again. Oh dear, I thought, how on earth can I get him the hell out of here. Suddenly Kees jumped on top of me. He fucked me as if his life depended on it. He yelled; do you feel something yet? I am sorry Kees but you are not inside of me. You are fucking my hand, for how long? This is not going to work. I decided to take matters in my own hands. I push Kees aside and start to massage his penis. Soon pimp Kees comes. Finally, great. He immediately jumps of the bed and looks at me. He told me it was cold. I sure satisfied you today didn't I Tien. You definitely did Kees. I was done with this. And he just lingered around trying to show off his body again. Okay Kees we are done for today. Bye bye. Okay, I will come back soon to fuck you real good, I want to spoil you. All right Kees; do practice at home will you; then it might work out. He walked out and I called out for him to bring more money next time. I will pay you nothing, I will come over to get your money, I am and will be your new pimp. Get the hell out of here Kees. Are you insane, find someone else. With your ridiculous ideas. Feeling slightly embarrassed Kees walked away. Great that's over. He will try to do this again but it's too late. He blew his job interview and unfortunately will never be hired.

Martine

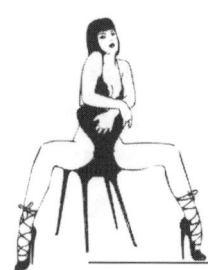 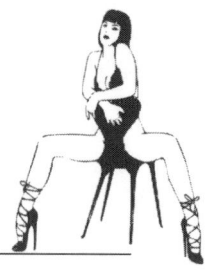

Our New Place Amsterdam

Good morning Oudenieuwstraat. Today I am going to look for a new place because it it time I got back to work. I need to make some money. We are too poor at the moment. For years I had been working at Katja's place. She had rented the whore house from a family who had another whorehouse at the Singel. Katja lived on the first floor. With Dick. She was always working early in the mornings. And I could start at nine. They were good times. But unfortunately all good things come to an end. Katja had gotten ill and to make matter worse she fell down the stairs. She ended up in the hospital, and after a couple of weeks she died. That's when everything began to change. The family who had to take care of everything had never understood her line of business so they had no idea what to do with the place. All they did was comment on it. You couldn't do one thing right. So they wanted me out and replaced me with two friends. Who made the place look better. After years of hard work I was out on the streets. That is why I was looking for a new brothel. After having asked Kittie multiple times I was ready to try again. I wanted to see if I could make it work this time. I worked for weeks to get back to the Oudenieuwstraat.

I rang Kittie's doorbell and she opened the window. She looked at me; what do you want? Excuse me, but you are renting a room aren't you? So; she snapped at me. This was going great. Well, I wanted to ask if the room was still available. The sign which says room available is still there. Okay well why don't you come on up first. We'll see. With a rope Kittie opened the door. I walked inside and up the steep stairs. I entered her room. Sit down on the couch. Would you like some coffee? I would love some. Her maid was there as well. The three of us drank a cup of coffee. Soon she brought out a cookie jar. The cookies looked delicious. Within no time the cookie jar was empty. Soon Kittie started talking about the rules. First of all; you need to work six days a week at the whore house; understood. Yes Kittie, when can I start? Tomorrow. Okay let's go downstairs. I will show you your room and explain how everything works. She walked down the stairs and I followed her. We walked into the room. It was peculiarly decorated with old fashioned lampshades with red light. An old fashioned dresser with small rugs on them. A large bed with a bedspread covered in flowers. A large closet; to put all my stuff. It was a great room, a shower and toilet were next to the room. It was very clean. Curtains white as snow, I take it all in and sink into the flower carpet. It felt good. The atmosphere was great. Well, what do you think? It's great. Well, I am Kittie and I will accept absolutely nothing, so don't screw up okay. They don't all come here to this whorehouse to work. That's okay, I understand Kittie. I shook her hand and left. I was happy I could start working tomorrow. I went home gathered all my sex toys and work stuff and put it in a bag. I spent the rest of the day with my family. I went to bed early and was ready to go the minute I woke up. I felt like I was going to a party. Quickly I went to work and rang the doorbell at Kittie's place. With a lot of noise she opened the window and yelled; oh it's you Tien. Yes, I am ready. I will open the door for you and come down. She came downstairs and greeted me.

Well, girl grab your things. She gave me another tour of the place. She greatly emphasized what was and what wasn't allowed. You'll be fine right? I will go back upstairs. Do you want some coffee, I would love some; okay I will bring you some in a minute. I turned on the radio and opened the curtains. Let them come. Let's get this party started. There are already a couple of guys walking by. Soon Kittie comes down with come coffee and a biscuit. She joins me and together we look outside. Hey Tien look out for that guy over there. Which one? The one with the long gray coat. Oh now I see him. What does he do? He will tell you the most amazing stories, that he will do anything for you and pay to get you out of this life. Oh I know the type; and he also works as a flasher. Climaxing right in front of your door. Bring him on, he is mine. Bye Tiem. Kittie walked back upstairs and soon afterwards a man approaches me. How much does it cost? I tell him how much and he follows me in. You are new here right? Yes I just started today.

I closed the door and he introduced himself as Peeter. I am Tiem. He pays me and I immediately get to work.

We are standing in the middle of the room while the radio is playing a love song. Peeter wraps his arms around me and we dance through the room. We end up on the bed and Peeter wants to stay put. Okay whatever he wants. Still holding each other I wank his largest finger; until he comes. Yes. Yes. And Peeter is done for the day. Miss I need to go, duty calls. It was great, thank you for the company. Now I need to go buy some groceries. By my sweet Martine. I want to see you again soon. That was a great start to my day. It was great at my new place.

Martine

Pimp Turd Amsterdam

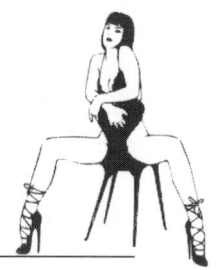

II was working at the Oudezijdsvoorburgwal. I was reading a book in between customers. Suddenly the M.C. sports car stopped in front of the brothel, with Mary and her pimp in it. She got out of the car and started yelling at him, kicked his car and walked in still screaming. Immediately she began to yell at me that I needed to get of her chair. In a minute when you are ready to start you work, that's how we always do it. Not anymore she yelled and grabbed a hold of me. Hey cut that out will you, just because you are fighting with your guy doesn't mean you should take it out on me. Suddenly she took hold of my hair and started pulling it. 'LET GO, LET GO' I yelled. But she didn't let go and pulled a little harder. That's when I started to hit her a couple of times and sat down on top of her. You will never do that to me again you bitch. Sometimes you just need to spread your legs girl, when it comes down to it. Suddenly she began to cry, what the hell is this. Just listen to me, all right tell me. I hadn't made enough money yesterday. Just get back to work Mary otherwise you won't have enough money again tonight according to that turd of a pimp of yours. Soon the Madame came downstairs carrying a large tray with coffee and treats. Say Tien what was up with all that noise just now? I just got out of the shower. Well,

Mary was upset because I was still sitting on her throne. It was ten to seven and I could sit on it until seven. Sometimes it takes a little longer with a customer, you do need to treat them well, and you can work that out together right? She had a fight with her pimp, and I got the most of it. Come one girls, let's get some coffee and a biscuit. We talked about it during our coffee break and everything was sorted out. Well, girls have fun, and good luck. Thank you Leen. I walked outside and leaned against the wall. Soon I saw a regular approach me. I know his rituals so I know what is about to happen, especially since he never changes. So I put myself on auto with Max. Tien how are you? I am great Max, put your clothes on the chair. Tien, today I will keep my clothes on. Just lie down on the bed Max. I sit down beside him, open his zipper put a condom on and start rubbing his boner, he is enjoying it with his eyes closed. Soon I pick up the pace and pull a little harder and faster because I have had enough with horny Max, and just like that he comes while softly moaning. Well, that's that. We clean ourselves up and look wonderful. We talk about the weather and walk outside. Max walks over to his bike and cycles away.

Martine